GOOD ADVICE
FOR A BAD ECONOMY

GOOD ADVICE
FOR A BAD ECONOMY

JOHN VENTURA
AND **MARY REED**

BERKLEY BOOKS, NEW YORK

B

A Berkley Book
Published by The Berkley Publishing Group
A division of Penguin Putnam Inc.
375 Hudson Street
New York, New York 10014

Copyright © 2003 by John Ventura and Mary Reed
Book design by Tiffany Kukec
Cover design by Pyrographx

PRINTING HISTORY
Berkley trade paperback edition / January 2003

Visit our website at
www.penguinputnam.com

Library of Congress Cataloging-in-Publication Data

Ventura, John.
Good advice for a bad economy / John Ventura and Mary Reed.
p. cm.
ISBN 0-425-18826-4
1. Finance, Personal.   I. Reed, Mary.   II. Title.

HG179 .V462 2003
332.024'02—dc21
2002028183

PRINTED IN THE UNITED STATES OF AMERICA

10   9   8   7   6   5   4   3   2   1

To Mary Ellen, my wife,
who loves me just the way I am.
—John

To Stacy, my "fourth sister," who has shown me
what grace under pressure is all about.
—Mary

CONTENTS

ACKNOWLEDGMENTS

I want to acknowledge my writing partner, Mary Reed, who also happens to be my best friend. She cares about the work and she cares about us. I also want to acknowledge the wind chimes I hear in the background when I talk to her on the phone. They catch the breeze on her porch as she works and it reminds me that someone has found a way to live sanely in this world, and I'm glad it's her.

INTRODUCTION

Not all that long ago, you probably never imagined that you would ever need a book like this. After all, you were enjoying the biggest economic boom in history and making plenty of money—maybe more than you ever dreamed of. Whenever you wanted to change jobs, there were plenty of well-paying opportunities to pick from. You could afford a new car, and maybe you even bought a second one "just for fun." You put an addition on your home or traded up to a bigger one, and you took nice family vacations. Meanwhile, the value of your 401(k) grew by leaps and bounds and your stock options guaranteed you a comfortable retirement. In fact, you may even have been a millionaire—on paper anyway. Although you spent a lot and saved a little, you didn't feel irresponsible given current economic conditions and predictions for the future. Plus, you worked hard for your money, so why not enjoy it?

But suddenly, almost in the blink of an eye, things began to change. The bottom dropped out of the technology sector, creating negative ripple effects throughout the economy. The stars of the "new economy," as well as reliable corporate citizens of the "old economy," began scaling back and laying people off. Some companies even filed for bankruptcy. The cushy bonuses and hefty salary increases you took for granted screeched to a halt, sales commissions shrunk, there were fewer opportunities for advancement, the value of your stock options plummeted, and the unthinkable happened—your 401(k) lost money.

The heady sense of financial invulnerability and exuberant optimism you used to take for granted is gone now, replaced by worry about your mounting debt and shrinking income, regret that you spent too much and saved too little during the boom, and concern for your family's financial future. Now, there never seems to be enough money to go around each month and you realize that just one big setback—like the loss of your job—could spell financial disaster. You feel helpless. How do you stabilize your financial situation so it does not go from bad to worse? What should you do about all of the money you owe to your creditors? What can you do to help yourself feel financially safe again?

Good Advice for a Bad Economy offers practical, gimmick-free, no-nonsense advice and information about how to spend money wisely, pinch pennies, manage your debts, and resolve your money-related problems. It helps you regain your sense of financial security by telling you how to put the brakes on your spending, live on what you make, negotiate with your creditors, and rebuild your finances once your money troubles are over. The book explains the laws that can protect you when you are selecting a credit card, shopping for a loan, trying to correct errors in your credit record, and it explains what to do when a company breaks one of those laws. It also advises you about when bankruptcy may be your best option and explains how the bankruptcy process works.

This book is divided in to three sections: Getting It Together, SOS and Looking Toward a Brighter Future. The first section tells you how to gain and maintain a positive attitude when you are overwhelmed by worries about money, how to size up the state of your finances, and how to set up a household budget. It also explains what bills to pay when you can't pay them all; provides lots of money-saving ideas; and reviews your options for increasing your household income, including finding a new job, getting more education, changing careers, and making extra money on the side. The Getting It Together section also gives you the legal lowdown on your debt collection rights, tells you how to negotiate with your creditors, explains the benefits of debt consolidation, and reviews the pros and cons of each option.

The SOS section provides must-have information about how to handle financial emergencies like evictions, foreclosures, and vehicle repossessions. It also explains when bankruptcy is appropriate, discusses the benefits and drawbacks of filing, and walks you through a Chapter 13 and a Chapter 7 bankruptcy so you can decide, in consultation with a bankruptcy attorney, which one is best for you.

Looking Toward a Brighter Future is the last section of this book. It explains why having a good credit record is important and how to correct credit record errors. It also guides you through the credit rebuilding process and tells you how to spot bogus credit repair firms.

The appendix highlights a wide variety of resources that can help you improve your finances and provide you with additional information. The resources include books and other publications, Web sites, government agencies, nonprofit organizations and businesses.

Good Advice for a Bad Economy gives you the information you need to take charge of your financial life, avoid expensive mistakes, and create a brighter financial future for yourself and your family. It recognizes that having enough money to pay your bills, to get through unexpected emergencies, and to achieve your financial goals makes life easier and more enjoyable in every way.

GETTING IT TOGETHER

1

FEELING SAFE

AGAIN

Losing your sense of financial security can be unsettling and downright scary. Things that you have always taken for granted, like being able to pay your bills and having enough money to provide yourself and your family with everything you need or want, are no longer guaranteed. As a result, you may be so preoccupied by worry about money that you can't sleep at night, have a hard time focusing during the day, and feel irritable and anxious all of the time. Feeling that way is understandable, because not having enough money is no fun and it makes life a lot more difficult. But, with patience, commitment, hard work, and a positive attitude, you can turn your situation around and create a brighter financial future. Maintaining that attitude can be a challenge, however, when you are staring at a stack of unpaid bills and have little or nothing in savings. Therefore, this chapter tells you how to gain and maintain the kind of can-do attitude that will sustain you through financially difficult times and keep you motivated and focused as you work to improve your situation and to regain a sense of financial safety. It also provides advice for keeping your money troubles in perspective, offers suggestions for alleviating your stress and worry, and highlights resources you can turn to if your money troubles begin taking an emotional toll on you and on your important relationships.

This chapter also asks you to examine your relationship with money—the role that money plays in your life as well as how you manage (or don't manage) your finances. When you had plenty of money to spend, your relationship with money may not have seemed worth thinking about, but, in fact, that relationship may have helped create the money troubles that you now face. Furthermore, unless you change it, the relationship may undermine your efforts to improve your financial situation and make long-term financial stability impossible to achieve.

Outlook Is Everything

It is tough to feel upbeat and positive when everything in your life is colored by money worries. Over time those worries can wear you down, fill you up with self-doubt, and leave you feeling hopeless and helpless. Also, if job loss has caused your financial situation to go downhill, your self-esteem may be at an all-time low, making it even more difficult to feel hopeful and in control of your life. Therefore, if you need an attitude adjustment to gain the courage and the resolve that are essential to taking charge of your financial situation and to moving forward, here are some suggestions for things to think about and things to do:

● Acknowledge that you have the power to improve your life. Yes, things may be difficult right now, but *you* can make them better. Think back on other challenges you have faced in life and remember how you dealt with them. They may also have related to your finances, to your health, an important relationship, your professional life, or to something else. Draw strength from your memories and apply the lessons you learned from past challenges to those you face now.

● Remind yourself that everyone has setbacks and disappointments in life—it is part of being a human being. All you have to do to confirm that fact is read the biography of a famous person or watch *Biography* on A&E. Everyone who has achieved success of any sort faced setbacks along the way.

● Rethink your concept of success. No doubt about it, having enough money to pay your bills and to pay for the things you and your family want or need makes life easier and a lot more fun. Even so, it is important that you keep money in perspective and that you not place too much value on it. How much money you have, the kind of car you drive and the size of your home are not the only ways to measure success and to create happiness in your life. In fact, in the grand scheme of life, those kinds of things are relatively meaningless, not to mention, short lasting. Real success and happiness comes from the quality of your relationships, the values you live by, your willingness to give to others, your ability to create a full and balanced life for yourself, et cetera. In the end, money cannot buy any of those things. When you put material possessions and a big salary in perspective, you will feel less anxious about your financial situation and you will be less apt to do things that will make your situation worse—fall for a get-out-of-debt-quick scam for example. In addition, your perspective will make it easier to give up or sell assets if doing either of those things is essential to resolving your financial problems.

● Don't get stuck in the past. You can't move forward if all you do is think about what you used to have and the way your life used to be, because you will be focusing all of your energy on the past. Sure, you have a right to yearn for the days when you were not worried about money, but don't let yourself get bogged down thinking about them. Stay focused on the future, but also find things to appreciate about your life today.

● Believe in a different dream. It may be hard to accept right now, but your money problems may actually be a blessing in disguise. As you work your way through them, you may create a happier, simpler, less stressful, more meaningful life for yourself and your family. Therefore, be open to change, don't resist it. Accept the changes that are happening in your life and acknowledge that you have the power through your attitude and your efforts to determine exactly where those changes will take you.

● Stay active. Exercise is a great way to take your mind off your worries, to feel better about yourself, and to guarantee yourself a good night's sleep. So, get off the couch! Jog, walk, lift weights, ride a bike, climb a mountain, play basketball with friends. Sweat your worries away. See the Stress Beaters for other suggestions for alleviating worry and stress.

● Help others. Volunteering your time to help those in need can help you feel good about yourself and can help you put your problems in perspective.

● Look for excuses to laugh. There is nothing like a good laugh for helping you get and keep a good attitude toward life. So, rent a funny movie, hang out with a witty friend, read the comics every Sunday, watch your favorite sitcom, or visit one of these comedy Web sites: *www.modernhumor.com* or *www.bluedonut.com*. Put a smile on your face!

● Have fun. Money worries don't have to mean an end to fun, just an end to expensive fun. With a little imagination you can come up with lots of ways to have a good time for little or no expense. Here are a few: do puzzles, play board games, take a walk with a friend, read a good book, invite your friends over for a potluck meal, work in your garden, participate in free or low-cost events in your community, go to the movies during off hours or rent videos, explore your local parks, take a drive in the country, take up a hobby you used to enjoy, et cetera.

Stress Beaters

Feeling stress is totally normal when you are worried about money, afraid of losing your job, or frustrated because you can't find a new one. However, too much stress is physically and emotionally draining. Therefore, if you are feeling too much stress—you can't sleep, you are having a hard time focusing, you are drinking more, you are extremely irritable, you are crying a lot—look for healthy ways to relieve the stress so that you can devote all of your energies to resolving your difficulties. The following ideas are all great ways to beat stress:

• Exercise. It's a fact: Vigorous exercise releases mood-elevating hormones. Although it may be tough to get started on an exercise program when you are feeling too much stress, you will feel better if you do.

• Learn to meditate.

• Take a yoga class.

• Listen to relaxing music.

• Work in your garden.

• Spend time with your friends.

• Take up a new hobby like painting, drawing, pottery making, woodworking, and so on. Learning something new can take your mind off of your problems and can also give you a sense of accomplishment when you feel down because you can't pay all of your bills or because you have lost your job. If you have lost your job, achieving something positive can give you a better outlook on life.

• Join a book group.

• Volunteer with a local charity.

• Help out at your child's school.

• Spend more time with your children.

- Enjoy the beauty around you—the sun rising or setting, flowers in a garden, the sound of water, the feel of a breeze, the warmth of the sun on your face, et cetera.

Katie Murphy is a prime example of someone who did not let a job loss and financial trouble beat her down. Instead, she used her resources and maintained a positive attitude and found a rewarding career in the process. Katie earned a good income, lived in a hip downtown neighborhood, and enjoyed spending money with her friends. She was not worried about how much credit card debt she had or the fact that there was just five hundred dollars in her savings account. She figured that her income would increase as she moved into better and better jobs and she promised herself that she would use some of her salary to pay off her debts and build up her savings. Then, the unthinkable happened. Katie lost her job. At first she could not believe what had happened to her, but after about a week she decided to face facts and figure out what to do next. Her first move was to call her parents to ask them if they would lend her money so she could pay her bills while she looked for a new job. Her parents had always been generous with Katie, and Katie knew that they could afford to help her out. Meanwhile, she began collecting unemployment and volunteering for a local nonprofit that assisted homeless mothers and children. She figured that the volunteer work would help keep her spirits up since sending out resumes and going on job interviews would not take up all of her time every day and she was afraid that she would get depressed if she did not stay busy.

As time went on, Katie began to enjoy her volunteer experience more and more. It made her feel good about herself and reassured her that she was still a contributing member of society even if she did not have a job to go to every day. After a while, Katie began to think that she might prefer working for a nonprofit organization rather than returning to the private sector, even though it would mean that she would make less money. When an interesting job opened up at the nonprofit where she was volunteering, Katie decided to apply for it. Two weeks later, she was hired. Now, a year later, Katie looks back on her job loss as a blessing in disguise, although she does not make as much money as she used to and she had to move into a less expensive apartment as a result. She realizes that she would probably never have considered working for a nonprofit if she had not been laid off.

Share with Your Family Members and Seek Out Your Friends

It takes two to tango, and it will take both you and your spouse or partner to resolve your money problems. Therefore, if you are the one who takes the lead on money matters, be sure that your spouse or partner is fully aware of your financial concerns and that you involve her in your efforts to address them. If you try to go it alone, you may become angry and resentful. Furthermore, getting through difficult times together can strengthen your relationship.

If your financial problems have already begun to drive a wedge between you and your spouse or partner, try to calmly discuss why you are having problems getting along and what you can do to alleviate the tension between the two of you. Consider having this discussion outside your home, in a restaurant or coffee shop, because your emotions are less apt to get in the way when you talk with one another in a public place. Wherever you have your discussion, avoid finger-pointing and playing the blame game. Focus on solutions.

Schedule an appointment with a mental health professional if you and your spouse or partner are not able to have a calm discussion about your finances. When you are having money troubles, the last thing you need is a relationship in turmoil. If you do not have insurance to cover mental health care, there may be a nonprofit mental health center in your community that offers its services for little or no money.

If your money problems are serious, don't try to hide them from your older children, but avoid scaring them by sharing every little detail. Your children probably sense that things have changed, and as a result they may be feeling anxious because they do not know why the changes have occurred or how they may be affected.

Don't let stress, worry, or embarrassment and shame about your money problems isolate you from your family and friends. You need them now more than ever. They can offer emotional support and a soft shoulder to lean on whenever you need it. Furthermore, the process of sharing what you are going through may deepen your relationships.

If you are afraid to let people know what is happening in your life because you don't want them to see you as a failure or because you don't want them to feel sorry for you, take a chance and share anyway. You may discover that they have experienced the very same problems you now face or that they are dealing with their own money problems. They may welcome the opportunity to share their worries and concerns with you and to trade ideas and resources for getting through financial tough times. On the other hand, if any of your friends reject you because of your money troubles, you have learned something important about them, painful as the lesson may be. Some friends are good-time friends only.

Examine Your Relationship with Money

When your finances have taken a turn for the worse, it is easy to blame your problems on other people or to chalk them up to bad luck. Although some finger-pointing may be appropriate, don't overlook the role you may have played in helping to create them. Unless you are willing to take a hard look at yourself and to make any changes that may be necessary, you risk repeating the same money mistakes over and over again, and condemning yourself and your family to a lifetime of financial ups and downs. Therefore, rather than automatically viewing yourself as an innocent victim of circumstances or of other people's mistakes, step back and ask yourself if any of the descriptions on the following list apply to you. Ask your spouse or partner or a friend to review the list as well. If any of them do apply and you need help to change the way you relate to money or to improve your money management skills, refer to the resources on page 14–16.

● **You have a "live for today, forget about tomorrow" attitude toward money.** That kind of attitude leads to using credit too much and saving too little. If you are young, you may rationalize your attitude by telling yourself that you have lots of time to plan for tomorrow, but right now you just want to have fun. You figure that once you are ready to be a more responsible money manager, it won't take long at all for you to whip your finances into shape. Sooner or later, you tell yourself, you will get out of debt and build up your savings, but too often "sooner or later" comes too late.

● **You spend to "keep up with the Joneses."** In our image-oriented society, we tend to be judged by the car we drive, the clothes we wear, and how freely we spend. Therefore, if being part of the crowd and looking successful is important to you, using credit to convey the right image can quickly become a habit. However, unless you are willing to live life on your own terms and be judged for who you are and not for what your money, or rather credit cards, can buy, you will never get out and stay out of debt.

● **You are addicted to credit.** Credit card issuers love people like you! They will even reward you for charging a lot by increasing your credit limits so you can wrack up even more credit card debt. Credit card issuers don't care if you can only afford to pay the minimum due on your debt each month. After all, the bigger your balances and the longer you take to pay them off, the more money they make off you.

● **You spend to cope with life.** When you use money to make yourself feel better because you are depressed, lonely, disappointed, or just plain bored, you end up in a vicious and costly cycle, just like people who cope with life by drinking or eating too much. However, once the good feelings you get from spending go away, you must spend again to get them back.

● **You have poor money management skills.** If you are like most consumers you never learned about money in school, and if your family was like most families in this country, your parents never discussed personal finance matters with you at home. So, when you graduated from high school or college, you opened a checking account, got a fist full of credit cards, and managed the best you could. Now, your lack of money management know-how has caught up with you.

● **Managing your money is not a priority in your life.** If you are like most people, you lead an extremely busy life and the demands of work and family leave you with little time for yourself. Therefore, even if you know how to manage your money, the last thing you feel like doing when you have free time is balance your checkbook, or monitor your budget. Yet, those simple tasks are essential to staying in control of your finances and to nipping money problems in the bud, when they are easier and less expensive to fix.

Resources That Can Help You

This list includes resources that can help you cope with your emotions when you are worried about money and struggling to pay your bills, as well as resources that you can turn to when you want to improve your money management skills. Most of them are free or low cost.

• *Mental health professionals*—If you are so depressed or anxious that you can't deal with your finances, if you have a spending problem, or if your money worries are creating problems in your relationship, schedule an appointment with a social worker, psychologist, or some other mental health professional.

If your insurance will not pay for the help, find out if there is a public or nonprofit mental health center in your area that offers the counseling you need at a price you can afford.

• *Debtor's Anonymous (DA)*—This organization uses the time-tested techniques of Alcoholics Anonymous to help people understand why they are addicted to spending and to help them get their spending under control. Look in your local phone book for the number of the DA chapter nearest you and begin attending its meetings. They are free and open to anyone. To benefit from DA all you have to do is show up. To learn more about DA go to the organization's Web site at *www.debtorsanonymous.org*, call 781-453-2743, or write to the organization at Debtors Anonymous, General Service Office, PO Box 920888, Needham, MA 02492-0009.

• *Consumer Credit Counseling Services (CCCS)*—This non-profit organization offers educational seminars as well as budgeting assistance and debt counseling for little or no cost. To find the CCCS office closest to you, call 1-800-388-2227. For more information about the services CCCS offers, go to chapter 5 in this book.

• *Your county cooperative extension service*—In many counties, this office offers budgeting and get-out-of-debt assistance. Find its number by looking in the government listings of your local phone directory.

• *Credit union and banks*—Some financial institutions offer periodic seminars on money management, debt, credit, and so on.

• *Military bases*—If you are in the military, the base you are associated with may offer money management counseling and education.

• *Local colleges*—Your area community college as well as other local educational institutions may offer money management classes as part of their continuing education programs.

2

TAKE CONTROL

The best way to alleviate your money worries is to take control of your financial situation by taking steps to improve it. Don't simply wait for your finances to get better on their own. They won't, unless you win a bundle in the lottery, hit it big on a TV game show, or inherit a fortune from a rich uncle. In fact, the longer you delay, the more your finances may deteriorate and the more difficult it will be to deal with them.

This chapter shows you how to take control. It explains how to assess the state of your finances by comparing your monthly household expenses to your monthly household income. Then it teaches you how to set up a household budget so you can control your spending and live on what you make. Both steps are essential to resolving your money problems and to regaining a sense of financial safety, regardless of whether those problems are relatively minor or whether you are drowning in debt. Improving your financial situation may also require that you make more money, negotiate with your creditors, consolidate your debts, and maybe even file for bankruptcy. Subsequent chapters in this book explain each of these other steps.

This chapter also provides advice about other actions you can take now to prepare for a possible job loss as well as a list of things to do right away if you do get the ax.

Follow the Money

At the end of each pay period do you scratch your head and wonder "Where did it all go?" The only way to answer that question is to identify all of your monthly expenses and then compare your total monthly spending to your total household income. This is an essential first step when you want to take control of your finances.

Record your spending information using the Expense and Income Worksheet on page 22. Modify the worksheet as necessary to reflect your particular expenses.

To begin figuring out where your money goes, locate your check registers, account statements, receipts, ATM receipts, and any other spending data you have for the past twelve months. If you are married or have a partner and you maintain separate checking accounts, ask your spouse or partner to pull together the same information for the same period of time. By category of expense, total up how much you spent on each expense item during those twelve months. Groceries, housing, transportation, credit card payments, utilities, and insurance are all examples of expense categories.

To get an accurate accounting of where your money is going, carry a small notebook with you everywhere you go for the next month and record every expense using the same expense categories as are on your worksheet. Your spouse or partner should do the same thing. This exercise is especially helpful for highlighting the amount of money you spend on miscellaneous stuff, no matter how small—spending that might not show up in your check registers or account statements because you paid for the items with cash.

Tracking your expenses this way can be a real eye-opener. You may be surprised to see how much your incidental expenses amount to. For example let's assume that each workday you purchase one latte for $3.50 and spend an average of $5 on lunch. On a monthly basis your spending on those two items adds up to $170. When you multiply that amount by 12 to calculate how much you spend in a year on lunch and lattes, it totals a whopping $2,040, and all you will have to show for your money may be a few extra pounds.

When you fill out the expense section of the worksheet, don't overlook any expenses that you are not paying right now because you don't have enough income. The goal of this exercise is to develop a full and accurate picture of *all* your expenses, so record every one. Also, if you are making monthly contributions to a savings or investment fund (e.g. savings account, IRA, mutual fund, etc.), record that amount on your worksheet as well under Monthly Contributions.

Not All Expenses Are Alike

Before you begin filling out the expense section of the worksheet, notice that it divides your expenses into three major categories: fixed, variable, and periodic expenses.

Fixed expenses stay the same from month to month. Common examples include: rent or mortgage payments, monthly health insurance payments, car payments, payments on other loans, child support payments, and so on.

Variable expenses change from month to month. Most of them tend to be discretionary expenses, which means that from month to month you have control over how much you spend on them. Your variable expenses may include: groceries, eating out, credit card payments, clothing, coffee, alcohol, sodas, cigarettes, dry cleaning, and gas for your car.

Periodic expenses come up just once in a while. They can be fixed or variable and may include: life and car insurance payments, home maintenance expenses, memberships, tuition, quarterly tax payments if you are self-employed, and so on. Depending on your situation, some of the expenses that are listed on the worksheet under the Periodic Expenses heading may actually be variable expenses for you or vice versa. Modify your worksheet as necessary.

After you have pulled together all of your spending data and have calculated annual totals for all of your expense categories, divide the totals by 12 to get monthly spending amounts for each. Then record those amounts on the worksheet under the heading Monthly Spending, add up all of your monthly spending totals, and record the grand total on your worksheet where it says Total Monthly Expenses.

Tally Your Income

Now total your household's net monthly income. For most of you that is your monthly salary less all deductions. Most of you can find that dollar amount by looking at your recent pay stubs, or at your last bank statement if your paychecks are direct deposited into your account. If your spouse or partner is employed, add his/her net monthly income to yours.

Account for any other regular income your household may receive, such as alimony or child support, government benefits, rental income, income from a family business, et cetera. If some of that income is periodic, not monthly, add up how much you receive over a year's time and then divide the total by 12 to come up with a monthly dollar figure. Add this other income to the total of your household's take-home pay.

If you are self-employed and your income varies from month to month, calculate an average monthly amount by dividing the net income figure on your most recent tax return by 12. However, if your business revenues have slowed since you filed that return, lower the monthly average income figure somewhat so you do not overstate how much you are making now. Examine your monthly business revenues and expenses since the return was filed to help you figure out by how much you should lower your monthly average income amount.

Once you have a dollar figure for your household's Total Net Monthly Income, record that amount on your worksheet. Then add up your Total Monthly Expenses and Contributions and subtract that total from your Total Net Monthly Income.

How do the two totals compare? If you end up with a negative number, your total monthly expenses are greater than your monthly income. If the number is positive, your expenses are less than your income. The next sections of this chapter discuss what to do next depending on the results of your expense and income comparison.

EXPENSE AND INCOME WORKSHEET

MONTHLY SPENDING

FIXED MONTHLY EXPENSES

(expenses that are the same every month)

Mortgage or rent	$_____
Car loan	$_____
Installment loans	$_____

Insurance

Health	$_____
Auto	$_____
Homeowners/renters	$_____
Life	$_____
Other	$_____

Total for Insurance	$_____
Memberships	$_____
Cable	$_____
Internet service	$_____
Child care	$_____
Children's allowances	$_____
After-school activities for children	$_____
Out-of-pocket medical expenses	$_____
Transportation (tolls, bus fare, parking, etc.)	$_____
Child-support payments	$_____
Alimony	$_____

MONTHLY SPENDING

VARIABLE EXPENSES

(expenses that vary from month to month)

Utilities $_____

Phone $_____

Cell phone $_____

Groceries $_____

Gasoline $_____

Credit cards $_____

Clothing $_____

Meals Out

  Breakfasts $_____

  Lunches $_____

  Dinners $_____

Total for Meals Out $_____

Alcohol $_____

Cigarettes $_____

Entertainment $_____
  (video rentals, movies, golf
    fees, etc.)

Makeup and toiletries $_____

Books and magazines $_____

Dry cleaning and laundry $_____

Cleaning supplies $_____

Gifts $_____

MONTHLY SPENDING

Church/charitable gifts $_____

Other $_____

PERIODIC EXPENSES
(occasional expenses)

Tuition $_____

Haircuts, manicures,
    pedicures, etc. $_____

Gifts $_____

Property taxes $_____

Auto registration and license $_____

Home repairs $_____

Subscriptions $_____

TOTAL EXPENSES: $_____

MONTHLY CONTRIBUTIONS

Savings $_____

Other $_____

**TOTAL EXPENSES &
CONTRIBUTIONS:** $_____

Total Net Monthly Income: $_____

**Total Net Income Less Total
Expenses & Contributions:** $_____

Surplus or Deficit: $_____

If Your Income Is Greater Than Your Expenses

You have enough income to pay your bills right now if your monthly household income is greater than your monthly expenses. Phew! However, don't rest on your laurels quite yet. Like many consumers who pay all of their bills every month, you may be just a catastrophe away from serious money troubles. For example, if you have a lot of debt relative to your income, especially high interest debt, and if you can only afford to make minimum due payments on your credit cards, you are in a precarious financial position. Your situation is even more precarious if you have little or nothing in savings.

How much is too much debt? Lenders would answer that question by comparing your finances to traditional income/debt ratios:

- Your total monthly debt payments—housing, credit card debt and other consumer debt—should not exceed 36 percent of your gross monthly income (income before taxes and other deductions).

- Your total monthly debt payments minus your monthly housing expense should be 20 percent or less of your gross monthly income.

- Your monthly mortgage payments (including insurance and property taxes) or your rent payments should be no more than 28 percent of your gross monthly income.

If your ratios are higher than what lenders like to see, reductions in spending are probably in order.

A savings account is your financial safety net. Without money in savings, you may have to use credit to help cover an unexpected expense, and if you lose your job, filing for bankruptcy may be the only way you can hold on to your important assets. Therefore, financial experts advise that you have six months worth of living expenses in savings, three months at the very least.

If you have too much debt relative to your income: Reduce your expenses and use the extra money to pay off your highest interest debt. Once you have that debt wiped out, pay off the debt with the next highest rate of interest, and so on. To pay down your high interest debts faster, make more money and apply the extra income to those debts and/or lower the interest rate on your debts by consolidating them. Chapter 4 discusses ways to make more money and chapter 5 reviews your debt consolidation options.

If you don't have enough money in your savings account: Reduce your spending and use the money that you free up to make your savings grow.

What to Do if You Are Operating at a Deficit

You face a bigger challenge if your expense and income worksheet shows that your total monthly expenses exceed your income. You may have been able to ignore this fact by using credit cards and cash advances to get by every month, but it's time to face facts: You are spending yourself into a hole, and month by month, that hole is getting deeper and deeper. Unless you figure out a way to dig yourself out, your financial situation will only get worse.

If your deficit is relatively small, all you may have to do to dig yourself out of debt is to reduce your spending. To find areas to cut, review the expense section of your worksheet. The expenses that need reducing may jump right out at you. If you need still more reductions, read chapter 3 for big and small money-saving ideas. After you have completed an initial round of spending cuts, revise your worksheet and then compare your total spending to your total income and also compare your new expense versus income figures to the debt-to-income ratios on page 25. If you need still more spending reductions, review your worksheet again and reread chapter 3.

If your deficit is substantial it may take several rounds of cuts before you can bring your spending in line with your income. (Use your worksheet to monitor the impact of each round.) However, you may have to do more than just reduce your spending to dig

Money$ense

If you have assets that you do not need or that you really can't afford to keep—an extra car or a recreational vehicle, real estate, et cetera—sell them and use the money to help pay off your highest interest debt.

yourself out of your financial hole. You may also have to:

- Negotiate new debt payment plans with your creditors.

- Consolidate your debt.

- Increase your income.

- File for bankruptcy, especially if you are in danger of losing your car and/or your home. Chapter 7 explains how bankruptcy works.

Make reducing your household spending a family affair, especially if you need to reduce your spending by a lot. Involving your family makes sense since the spending cuts are likely to affect everyone in your household one way or another. Furthermore, your family members will be less apt to resent any changes in their lifestyle that may result from your cost cutting if you ask them to help you figure out what expenses to reduce.

Involving your family has other potential benefits as well. For example, the full burden for improving your financial situation won't be on your shoulders. Another potential benefit is that you will have the opportunity to teach your children important lessons about money that they can then apply to their own lives when they become adults. Maybe if you had learned those same lessons when you were their age, you would not be worried about your finances now.

Create a Budget

After you have pared back your expenses as much as you can right now, set up a monthly budget for your family. The budget will reflect how you intend to allocate your income each month. It may take discipline to live on your budget, but sticking to it is essential and over time it will become easier to do. If you can't afford to pay all of your expenses, read What to Pay When You Can't Pay Everything later on in this chapter so you can be sure to allocate your limited dollars to the right things.

Money$ense

You can use the My Finances section of the Quicken Web site to track your expenses each month.

Use the Monthly Budget form on page 30 to create your

household budget, or set one up using budgeting software like Intuit's Quicken Deluxe. Microsoft's Money is another option. After your budget is set up and all of your information has been entered, the software makes it easy to review and update your budget each month.

Once you have set up your budget, post it on your refrigerator or in some other visible location as a regular reminder of how your household intends to allo-

Money$ense

Make living on a budget a habit for life, not just for difficult financial times. Living on a budget will help you make the most of your money and will make it easier for you to achieve important financial goals like buying a home, paying for your child's college education, taking a nice vacation, or funding your retirement. Living on a budget can also help you spot financial problems as soon as they develop, when they are easier to fix.

cate its money every month. Then at the end of each month compare how your actual spending that month compares to what you budgeted. Do this with your spouse or partner, and with your older children too if they want to be involved. Although you may find the budget review process about as much fun as a trip to the dentist, there is no sense in having a budget if you don't keep track of how well you stick to it.

If you find at the end of a month that your actual spending is greater than what was budgeted, try to figure out why and then decide what you can do to eliminate the overruns. You may have them because:

- Your budget is unrealistic.

- You had an unexpected expense.

- Your family is not 100 percent committed to living on a budget.

Be sure to revise your budget whenever you pay off a debt, consolidate debts, increase your income, or begin contributing more to savings.

MONTHLY BUDGET

MONTHLY SPENDING

TOTAL HOUSEHOLD INCOME: $_____

FIXED MONTHLY EXPENSES

Mortgage or rent $_____

Car loan $_____

Installment loans $_____

Insurance

    Health $_____

    Auto $_____

    Homeowners/renters $_____

    Life $_____

    Other $_____

Total Insurance Amount $_____

Membership $_____

Cable $_____

Internet service $_____

Child care $_____

Children's allowances $_____

After-school activities for
    children $_____

MONTHLY SPENDING

Out-of-pocket medical expenses $_____

Transportation $_____
  (tolls, bus fare, parking, etc.)

VARIABLE EXPENSES

Utilities $_____

Phone $_____

Cell phone $_____

Groceries $_____

Gasoline $_____

Credit cards $_____

Meals Out
  Breakfasts $_____
  Lunches $_____
  Dinners $_____

Meals Out Total $_____

Drinks $_____

Cigarettes $_____

Entertainment (video rentals,
  movies, golf fees, etc.) $_____

Clothing $_____

Makeup and toiletries $_____

Books and magazines $_____

MONTHLY SPENDING

Dry cleaning and laundry $_____

Cleaning supplies $_____

Other $_____

PERIODIC EXPENSES

Tuition $_____

Haircuts, manicures,
    pedicures, etc. $_____

Gifts $_____

Property taxes $_____

Auto registration and license $_____

Home repairs $_____

Subscriptions $_____

              TOTAL EXPENSES: $_____

MONTHLY CONTRIBUTIONS

Savings $_____

Other $_____

        TOTAL EXPENSES &
        CONTRIBUTIONS: $_____

      Total Net Monthly Income: $_____

Total Net Income Less Total Expenses
& Contributions: $_____

What to Pay When You Can't Pay Everything

When your monthly household income is not enough to cover all of your expenses, it is important to know which bills to pay and which ones to let slide. Don't simply pay the creditors who yell the loudest or who send you the most threatening letters. They may actually belong at the bottom of your bills-to-be-paid list.

Your rent or mortgage, utility bills, and groceries should be your priorities. Your family needs a roof over its head, gas and electricity to live comfortably under that roof, and food on their table. Other expenses that belong at the top of your list include:

- Property taxes and homeowners' insurance payments if you are a homeowner, assuming those expenses are not included in your mortgage payments.

- Car payments and car insurance, especially if you need your car to get to and from work or to interview for jobs.

- Child support payments, especially if they are court ordered.

- Income taxes. If you cannot pay everything that you owe to Uncle Sam, file a tax return anyway and ask for an installment plan or an Offer in Compromise. Don't simply ignore your tax obligation, because the IRS has extraordinary collection powers and can take just about anything it wants from you when you don't pay your taxes. Chapter 5 explains how installment plans and Offers in Compromise work.

- Student loans. If you fall behind on your federal student loans, the IRS may intercept your tax refunds or your employer may be ordered to take money out of your paychecks to help pay off your student loans. For more information on government student loans and what to do when you can't repay them, read chapter 5.

Watch Out!

Don't let the fear of losing credit or having a damaged credit record deter you from following the information in this section. Despite the negative consequences, not paying certain bills is the best way to deal with your finances when you don't have enough money to pay everything that you owe. Furthermore, once your money troubles are behind you, you can rebuild your credit so that you can obtain new credit. Chapter 9 explains the rebuilding process.

- Secured debts, assuming you do not want to lose the assets that collateralize those debts. The next section explains the difference between secured and unsecured debt.

- Health insurance payments, if you pay for your own insurance.

Depending on your circumstances and on your family's needs, other expenses may also belong on your list of top priorities. For example, if your child has a chronic illness that requires regular medical treatment, those medical bills should definitely be paid.

If you have any money left over after you have budgeted for your top-priority expenses, use it to pay off your unsecured debts, starting with your highest interest debt. The next section tells you what may happen if you fall behind on your unsecured debt payments.

Secured and Unsecured Debt

The money you owe to your creditors is categorized as either secured or unsecured debt. Like most people, you probably have both kinds of debt.

Secured debt is debt that you guarantee to repay by giving your creditor a lien on an asset that you own. That asset is called your "collateral." If you fall behind on a secured debt, the lien gives the creditor the right to take the collateral as payment. The more money you borrow, the more likely it is that you will have to secure the loan with collateral. However, a creditor may demand collateral even if you borrow a relatively small amount of money when your finances are shaky, if you have not had credit for very long, or when you are rebuilding your credit after money troubles. Home mortgages, home equity loans and car loans are common examples of secured debt.

Unsecured debt is debt that is not collateralized. Therefore, if you fall behind on an unsecured debt, the creditor is in a relatively weak

> **Money$ense**
>
> If you are in the military or if you are a Native American living on a reservation, you are protected from creditors' collection actions regardless of whether the creditor is trying to collect on a secured or an unsecured debt.

position because there is no collateral for it to take as payment. Also, if you file for bankruptcy, your unsecured creditors may end up with little or nothing. Credit card debt is the most common type of unsecured debt, but the money you may owe to a hospital or doctor, to a retailer, to your utility, phone company, Internet provider, or to a cable company are other examples.

When you fall behind on a relatively small unsecured debt, the creditor will probably send you at least one letter demanding that you pay up. If you don't, your account may be turned over to a debt collection agency. In the end however, if you don't pay, the creditor may write off the debt as "uncollectible," which means that it will stop trying to collect the debt.

If you owe a substantial amount of money to an unsecured creditor, the creditor may sue you to get the court's permission to garnish your wages or seize your bank account. However, state and federal laws place limits on how much a creditor can take from each of your paychecks and how much it can take from your bank account. Also, some states do not permit wage garnishment.

If you are sued by a creditor or a creditor threatens you with collection action, make an appointment with a consumer law attorney. Chapter 5 explains how a consumer law attorney can help you and provides you with resources for finding a good consumer law attorney in your area.

An unsecured creditor may also ask the court's permission to seize one of your assets so it can sell the asset and apply the proceeds to your debt. Or, the court may allow it to place a judgment lien on an asset that you own such as your home or

Watch Out!

If you default on a debt and your creditor reports the default to one or more of the national credit bureaus, that information will become part of your credit record. Federal law allows the default information to remain in your record for seven years. As long as that information is in your credit record, it will be difficult, if not impossible, for you to qualify for new credit, secured or unsecured, from a reputable company at reasonable terms. To learn more about credit bureaus, credit records, and how to rebuild your record after it has been damaged by money troubles, read chapters 8 and 9.

a piece of land. When it places a lien on your asset, the creditor is gambling that when you sell that asset it can take some of the sale proceeds. However, if other creditors already have liens on the same asset, that creditor may get nothing, since the creditors with the earlier liens are entitled to be paid first.

State property exemption laws may also stand in the way of an unsecured creditor taking your assets or placing judgment liens on them. Those laws bar creditors from seizing or selling certain assets, including some household goods, furniture, appliances and, depending on your state, your home and vehicle. Each state has its own exemption laws. To find out about the law in your state, talk with a consumer law or bankruptcy attorney. You can also get the information on the Internet by doing a search using the phrase, "state property exemptions" or "property exemptions in (your state)."

If all of your assets are exempt from collection action, and assuming that your wages cannot be garnished and the funds in your bank account cannot be taken because of your state's laws, you are probably "judgment proof." That means there is nothing that an unsecured creditor can do to collect what you owe. In that case, the debt will probably be written off as uncollectible.

What *Not* to Do When You Are Pinching Pennies

When money is tight, you may be so anxious to maintain the lifestyle that you have become accustomed to or to alleviate the pressure that comes from not being able to pay all of your bills that you end up doing things that will make your financial situation a lot worse and maybe even put you on the wrong side of the law. Therefore, here is a list of the things that you should not do when you are having money problems:

- Do not give a creditor a postdated check. You have no guarantee that the check will not be deposited before its date, which may cause the check to bounce, unless you have overdraft protection. If the check does bounce, your bank will charge you an insufficient funds fee, the business to whom you wrote the check will charge you a fee as well, and you will have to make good on the check or risk being prosecuted for passing a bad check.

- Do not write a check when there is not enough money in your account to cover it. You risk the same consequences as when you postdate a check.

- Do not lie to a creditor or make promises to a creditor that you cannot keep. If the creditor finds out that you have lied, your credibility will be shot, and later, if you contact that same creditor to try to negotiate a more affordable debt payment plan or to ask for some other concession, the creditor may not be inclined to work with you.

- Do not borrow money from a company that advertises loans to consumers who are having financial trouble. If you fall for the company's offer, you will be charged a very high interest rate and you may have to pay a substantial fee just to get the loan. Some of these companies encourage consumers to borrow more money than they can afford to pay back and require consumers to collateralize a loan with their car or their home. They are betting that the consumers will not be able to keep up with their loan payments and that they will be able to take their collateral as a result.

• Do not do business with a rent-to-own firm. Rent-to-own is an expensive way to purchase a new appliance, furniture, or nonessential items like a TV, VCR, and electronic equipment. By the time the rental period is up and the item is yours, you will have paid as much as three times more for the item than if you had waited until you could afford to purchase it with cash or with low interest credit. Furthermore, depending on the terms of the rent-to-own contract, missing just one payment may give the company the right to repossess the item you are buying and to keep all of the money that you have paid so far. That amount could be substantial if you are near the end of your contract.

• Do not get a payday loan, also called a cash-advance loan, check-advance loan, postdated-check loan, or a deferred-deposit loan. Whatever its name, a payday loan is a short-term, high interest loan usually made by a finance company or a check-cashing business. It is a very, very expensive source of fast cash, and given the way payday loans are set up, it is quick and easy to get deep in debt to a payday lender. Here is how a payday loan works: You write a personal check to the lender for the amount that you want to borrow plus the fee that the lender charges to give you the loan, and you agree to pay back the full amount of the loan on your next payday. The loan fee is usually a percentage of the loan's value or a set dollar amount for every $50 or $100 that you borrow. In return, the payday lender gives you cash for the amount of the check less the fee, and agrees not to cash the check but rather, to return it to you when you repay the loan. If you cannot afford to repay the loan on your next payday, you can roll over the loan; but you will have to pay the lender another fee, which will be higher than the first one you paid.

Preparing for a Possible Job Loss

If you are worried that you may lose your job and about how the loss will affect your finances, don't wait for the ball to drop to prepare for what may come. Start now by developing a contingency plan. Having the plan in place will help you feel less anxious about the future and more in control of your finances. Here are some suggestions for what you can do now to prepare:

- Keep $500, $1,000—the exact amount is not important—in a safe place just in case. If you need to move out of your apartment, you could use the money to pay the deposit on a new place to live, or if you are low on funds, you could use it to help feed your family.

- Develop a survival budget. Figure out how little you can live on.

- Build up your savings so that you have three, preferably six, months of expenses stashed away. This is your financial safety net.

- Stop using your credit cards.

- Pay more on your high interest debts, if you can afford to—but not at the expense of building up your savings.

- Don't make any large purchases unless they are absolutely necessary.

- Stock up on staples like beans, pasta, and rice.

- If there are just a few payments left on your car loan, pay it off. You may need to use the car as loan collateral if you decide that consolidating your debts is a good way to deal with your financial situation. Chapter 5 discusses debt consolidation.

• Meet with your financial advisor if you have one. The advisor can help you review your finances, figure out how to improve them, and help you determine whether any of your assets could provide you a ready source of cash if you needed it. The advisor can also review the pros and cons of tapping those assets for cash. If you have a lot of money invested in stocks, bonds, or mutual funds, meet with your broker too.

• Talk with your parents about whether you could move back in with them temporarily if you lost your job. Discuss all of the conditions of your moving back in. You may also want to ask if they would give you a loan should you lose your job and need

Watch Out!

If your parents do not have much money to spare and especially if they are close to retirement age, don't ask them for a loan. Many parents will help out their children even if it means that they have to do without.

the money to make ends meet. Chapter 5 discusses things to consider before you borrow from someone you know.

• Ask your employer to increase the number of income tax exemptions you are claiming so that less money will be withheld from your paychecks. Although this may increase the amount of income taxes you owe on April 15, if you lose your job and are out of work for a while, the loss of income will probably make up for the increased tax liability.

• Apply for a home equity loan or a home equity line of credit while you still have a job, but not unless you are absolutely sure that you can make the loan payments if you become unemployed. You may not be able to qualify for the loan after you are laid off and the loan money could be a lifesaver.

● Update your resume and start exploring your job options. Chapter 4 offers advice and resources for landing a new job.

Plan B: If the Ax Falls

Even when you know that your job may be in jeopardy, actually losing it is almost always difficult. However, getting through the experience is easier if you know ahead of time exactly what to do and what not to do when the ax falls. Therefore, to help you make smart decisions, use the following list to develop a plan of action that you can begin implementing as soon as you lose your job:

● Negotiate the best severance package you can. Be clear about what you are entitled to and then try to get more. Your employer may feel bad about having to let you go. Therefore, he/she may be willing to "sweeten the pot." Ask for a better severance package shortly after you find out that you have lost your job. The longer you wait, the less guilt your employer is likely to feel. Among other things, you may want to ask:

Money$ense

If you are offered the option of receiving your severance pay in installments rather than in a lump sum, take into account the stability of your employer. If you are not sure that the company will be around in a couple of months, take the money in a lump sum or you may never see it.

- For more severance pay.
- To stay on your employer's health plan longer.
- To be provided with outplacement services, including a phone and office, job counseling, and maybe even re-training, if you think you may want to change careers or if you know that increasing your job skills will make you more competitive in the job market. Ask for one month of outplacement services for every year you worked for your employer. Some employers automatically offer these services, especially when they are laying off a lot of employees.

● If your employer says that you are not entitled to severance pay, check your company's employee handbook or the details of any employment agreement you may have signed when you were hired to find out what they say about severance pay. Also, check with other employees you know in positions similar to yours who were let go to find out if they received a severance package and what was a part of the package. If you conclude that you should receive a severance package but your employer continues to refuse, contact an employment law attorney.

Watch Out!

Don't cash out your 401(k) or 403(b) unless you absolutely have to, because taxes and an early withdrawal penalty mean you will get considerably less than what is in the account now. A better option if you have at least $5,000 in the account is to leave it where it is until you get a new job. Then, you can transfer the funds into your new employer's 401(k). Another option is to set up an Individual Retirement Account (IRA), if you don't already have one, and ask your former employer to send the funds in your 401(k) or 403(b) to the financial institution that is holding the IRA.

● Be sure to get paid for any vacation time, bonuses, and commissions you may be entitled to. If you are leaving the company just prior to the time that you would be vested to receive stock options or to participate in your employer's pension plan, ask if your vesting period can be accelerated or if you can remain on your employer's payroll until you reach your vesting date.

● If your employer makes signing a noncompete agreement a condition of getting severance, be sure that the agreement is specific as to its duration and the companies that you cannot go to work for. Your employer may also want you to agree not to say bad things about the company after you leave as a condition of receiving severance. As a condition of signing, try to get your employer to agree to up the ante on the severance package.

● If you were fired from your job, talk with your employer about the best way to explain your departure to future potential employers. They are likely to ask for an explanation. Also, out of fear of being sued, many employers will only verify dates of employment, title, and salary when they are called about a former employee. Therefore, if you want your employer to provide a detailed reference, find out what he is willing to say about you to potential employers.

● Apply for unemployment benefits at your state unemployment office.

● Check out all of the services that your state employment services office has to offer. To link up with the Web site of that office in your state, go to *www.doleta.gov* and then click on "State One-Stop Web Sites."

● Update your resume and figure out the best way to replace the income you have lost. Chapter 4 reviews your options.

● If you already have a household budget, adjust it to reflect your loss of income and the amount of unemployment income you will be receiving. Also, use your budget to figure out if you can afford to pay all of your bills and to identify any expenses you can cut. If you don't have a budget, develop one following the process outlined in this chapter.

● Suspend contributions to your savings and retirement plans until you have reviewed your household budget and know whether or not you can afford to continue making them.

● Contact your creditors. Let them know that you have lost your job but are actively looking for a new one and ask if they would lower the interest rates on your cards—or even waive the interest—for a couple of months. If you have a good account payment history, your creditors may cooperate with you. Be sure to mention that history when you call your creditors however. Chapter 5 discusses various ways of dealing with your debts and creditors.

● Decide what to do about health coverage if you have been covered by your company's plan. One option is to get on your spouse's plan, if he/she has employer-provided health coverage. Another option is to remain on your employer's health plan through COBRA, a federal law that allows employees under certain conditions to remain on their employer's plan for a limited period of time. If you were a part of your employer's health plan for at least 18 months, your employer is legally obligated to notify you that you can remain on the plan for up to 18 months through COBRA. Your spouse and kids can too. You will have 60 days to opt for the coverage if you are interested. Only employers with at least 20 employees must offer COBRA coverage. The benefit of COBRA is that you have health coverage while you are looking for a new job, getting a business off the ground or shopping for other health coverage. However, COBRA coverage is expensive. Whereas before, your employer may have paid all or part of the cost of your health coverage, under COBRA, you must pay the full cost of the coverage, plus a two percent surcharge. A third option is to purchase a temporary insurance policy. However, the policy will probably only cover hospitalizations and other major medical care.

● Read the rest of this book.

3

TIGHTEN YOUR FINANCIAL BELT

This chapter offers lots of suggestions for saving money and a few money-making tips as well. All of the ideas are organized by category of spending—housing, groceries, insurance, travel, and so on. Some of the suggestions you read about will save you a little and will have a negligible effect on your lifestyle. Others will save you a lot but may also involve significant changes in the way you and your family live. Those changes may be necessary however if you can't live on what you make or if you know that you could not pay your bills if you lost your job or experienced some other serious financial setback.

How to Benefit the Most from This Chapter

Read this chapter with an open mind. Don't automatically dismiss any spending cut suggestions, especially if you have a lot of cost cutting to do. Also, don't ignore a suggestion just because it won't save you a bundle. Taken together, numerous small spending cuts can save you a substantial amount of money over time.

You and your family may have a difficult time adjusting to some of your reductions, especially if they involve giving up things that you enjoy or that you worked hard to get—nice vacations, expensive clothing, recreational vehicles, and so on. However, once your finances are looking up, you may be able to afford some of those things again.

When you are reducing your spending, try to focus on what you will gain from the cuts, not on what you have to give up. That perspective will make it easier to accept their impact on your life. For example, spending less may help you reduce any tension in your relationship with your spouse or partner that your money problems have helped to create, or it may help you hold on to your home or car. Your spending reductions may even teach you and your family new things about yourselves and one another. For example, you may discover that you are pretty good with a hammer and a wrench, and that you can handle your own simple car repairs. Your kids may find out that they don't miss the organized activities they had to give up as a result of your spending reductions and that they actually enjoy having more free time after school and on weekends. When all is said and done, you may conclude that living on less enriches, rather than diminishes, your lives as individuals and as a family.

When you read this chapter, keep a pen or pencil handy so that you can jot down any cost-saving ideas that may occur to you. Make notes in the margins of this book or in a notebook. Be sure to ask your spouse or partner to read this chapter too.

Stop Using Plastic

Using credit cards is convenient, but unless you pay off your card balances every month, they are an expensive way to pay for things. Yet, if you are like most American consumers, you have several credit cards in your wallet and each of them has a balance of at least a couple of thousand dollars. If you pay only the minimum due on those cards, you will be old and gray before you have the card balances paid off. Therefore, the first and easiest thing you can do to get your finances under control is to stop charging and start operating on a cash-only basis. Continuing to buy things with credit will only get you deeper into debt.

You should also get rid of all but one MasterCard or Visa bankcard, two at the most. There is absolutely no reason to have more than that. Unless you are extremely disciplined, the more cards you have, the more credit card debt you will rack up.

Keep the bankcard with the best terms of credit because it costs you the least to use. Formally cancel each account by writing to the customer service address on each of your bankcard billing statements. In your letters, ask that your account be closed and ask the bankcard company to tell the credit bureau or bureaus it reports to that the account was closed at *your* request. Cut up each cancelled credit card and throw them away.

Criteria for Comparing Credit Cards

Don't know which card to keep and which to cut up? Here are some guidelines to follow to determine which credit card is best.

The federal Truth in Lending Act (TLA) says that when you apply for a credit card (or for any kind of credit), or when a company sends you a credit card offer in the mail, the creditor must provide you with written information regarding the terms of the credit. That way you can figure out if the offer is a good deal or not. You can also get terms of credit information by looking at your bankcard billing statement or by calling the customer service number for your bankcard.

According to the TLA, creditors must provide the following information when you apply for a credit card or when you are offered one:

• *The card's periodic rate.* This is the rate of interest that you will have to pay each day on the card balance. The higher the rate, the more the balance costs you. The periodic rate is a particularly important term of credit if you know you will carry a balance on your credit card from month to month.

• *The card's annual percentage rate, or APR.* This is the card's periodic rate expressed as an annual rate, or the periodic rate multiplied by 365. An interest rate may not seem high when it is expressed as a periodic rate but it will appear substantially higher when it is expressed as an annual rate.

• *The card's grace period.* This is the amount of time that you will have to pay your credit card balance in full before you will be charged interest. The longer the grace period the better. If you intend to maintain a balance, watch out for credit cards that have no grace period. Also, avoid credit cards that charge interest even if you pay the full balance on your account during the grace period.

• *The card's balance calculation method.* Credit card companies use one of several different methods to calculate the amount of interest you have to pay on your card balance. Some methods are a lot more expensive than others. Ranked from best to worst for consumers, those methods are: Adjusted Balance, Average Daily Balance Excluding New Purchases, Previous Balance, Average Daily Balance Including New Purchases, Two Cycle Average Daily Balance Excluding New Purchases, and Two Cycle Average Daily Balance Including New Purchases.

• *The card's fees.* Some cards come with more fees than other cards or with higher fees. For example, you may be charged an annual or membership fee, a late fee, a fee for going over your credit card limit, a bounced check fee, an advance fee, and a balance transfer fee. Some credit card issuers even charge a transaction fee, which is a fee that you pay every time you use your card, or a fee for not using your card enough. Obviously, the best card is the one with the fewest and the lowest fees.

Credit card companies only have to give you 15 days' notice before they change the terms of your credit and there are few limits on the number of times that they can change the terms. Information about a change will probably be buried in the small print on a piece of paper that comes with your monthly statements. Some credit card companies will change your terms of credit if you are late paying what you owe to them or other creditors.

Money$ense

If you don't trust yourself not to use the bankcards you keep, put them in a plastic sandwich bag full of water and the bag in the freezer. Then, you will have to wait for the ice to thaw before you can use them. Hopefully, while the ice is thawing, you will change your mind about charging.

Cancel all of your retail credit cards as well. Not only do they come with a higher rate of interest than most MasterCards and Visas, but most businesses that issue their own credit cards also accept either or both of the national bankcards. Therefore, there is no reason to have a retail charge card. Get help if you can't stop using credit. You may have a spending problem. Until you deal with your problem, getting and staying out of debt will be difficult if not impossible for you to do. Chapter 1 highlights resources that can help you put the brakes on your spending.

Spending Less to Keep a Roof over Your Head.

Keeping a roof over your head is probably your single biggest expense when you take into account not just the amount of your monthly mortgage or rent payment but also the cost of heating and cooling the place where you live, keeping the lights on, and paying for repairs and maintenance. However, there are plenty of things you can do to reduce the cost of your housing. For example, if you own your home you can:

● Lower your house payments by refinancing your mortgage if interest rates are lower than when you got your mortgage. Read Chapter 5 for more information on refinancing.

● Rent out an extra room in your home or the garage apartment behind your home. Make sure that all prospective tenants complete a rental application. Check their references and verify their rental and employment histories. Once you have decided on a tenant, ask the tenant to sign a written lease agreement. The lease should clearly spell out your obligations as well as the tenant's and should obligate the tenant to pay at least one month's rent up front as a security deposit. You can purchase a standard rental application and lease agreement at your local office supply firm.

If the tenant will be living in your home, choose someone you will be compatible with and be clear with the tenant before he signs the lease about your expectations regarding noise, guests, use of the kitchen and other common areas, et cetera. Spell out your expectations in a written addendum to the lease.

Watch Out!

Before you begin the rental process, familiarize yourself with your legal obligations and rights as a landlord. For example, the federal Fair Housing Act prohibits you from discriminating against a prospective tenant on the basis of race, color, age, sex, national origin, religion, marital status, or an applicant's mental or physical disability. Check with your state and local government about any other laws you have to comply with as a landlord, including laws relating to repairs and evictions.

● Take advantage of the free or low-cost energy audits your local utility may offer. The energy auditor will look for ways to make your home more energy efficient so you can save money on your heating and cooling bills. Depending on what the auditor recommends, you may be able to implement his ideas yourself—caulking, weather stripping, insulating, and changing showerheads for example. Your utility may also offer rebate programs to help defray the costs of energy improvements as well as low interest energy loans through local banks.

● Enroll in your utility's load management or off-rate program.

● Consult *Consumer Reports* at *www.consumerreports.org* before you replace a major appliance to find out which brands and models combine an affordable price with high quality and energy efficiency. Then call several stores in your area to find out if they sell the brand and model you are interested in and how much they sell it for. Ask if the price they quote you over the phone is their best price. They may offer you a better deal.

● If your home needs repairing, don't sign a contract that requires you to pay the full cost of the repairs up front. Once the contractor gets your money you may never see him again. Also, when a repair involves a significant amount of money, always get written, fixed-price bids from several licensed, well-established contractors.

Watch Out!

If you can't afford to maintain your home and fix problems as they occur, it may be time to move. Problems like a leaky roof, peeling paint, faulty plumbing, stained carpeting, and damaged cabinets and countertops will affect your home's resale value and maybe even your ability to borrow against your equity.

● Rent out your home, assuming you can rent it for at least enough to cover your mortgage payments as well as the costs of property taxes and insurance. Then find a less expensive place to live in until you can afford to move back into your home.

● If your mortgage payments have become the proverbial albatross around your neck, consider selling your home, assuming you can sell it for enough to pay off the balance on your mortgage. If it sells for a lot of money, you may have enough for a down payment on a new, more affordable home.

To help you decide whether selling your home is a good idea, meet with a couple of real estate brokers. Find out how much they think you should ask for your home and how much similar homes in your neighborhood have sold for recently. Also, sit down with your CPA or financial advisor to help you decide if selling is a smart financial move. For example, if your home has appreciated a lot since you purchased it, you may end up owing a bundle in taxes, which could end up compounding your money problems.

If you are a renter, not a homeowner, suggestions for reducing your monthly housing expenses include:

● Get a roommate, assuming your lease allows you to have one. If it does not, speak to your landlord about changing your lease so you can have a roommate.

● Sublet the place you are renting. If your lease prohibits subleasing, tell your landlord why you would like to and ask if he would amend your lease to allow it. Chapter 6 discusses issues related to subleasing.

● Move to someplace more affordable. If you want to move before your lease is up, read your lease to find out the consequences of breaking it. If you stand to lose a substantial amount of money, you may be better off waiting to move until you have reached the end of your lease, assuming you can afford the rent payments. To help you decide what to do, read What to Do About Your Past-Due Rent in chapter 6.

Spending Less to Get from Here to There

After housing, your next biggest monthly expense is probably transportation, when you consider not just the amount of your car payments but also all of the other expenses that come with car ownership, including the cost of tags and registration, insurance, gasoline, maintenance and repairs. Therefore, here are suggestions for how to drive for less:

● Pump your own gas.

● Shop for the cheapest gasoline and don't buy a higher grade than you really need.

● Wash your own car.

● Check your vehicle's fluids periodically, keep your tires inflated to the appropriate pressure, and get your engine tuned regularly. These simple steps will keep your car running better, longer.

● Learn how to change your own oil and to do your own simple car repairs. Your local community college or a continuing education program at your area's university may offer classes on auto maintenance and repair. The AutoSite Web site at *www.autosite.com* is another helpful resource. It explains what is under your car's hood, helps you diagnose what is wrong with your vehicle when it is not running right, and tells you how to perform common repairs.

● Find an affordable, reliable mechanic before you need one. The mechanic should be licensed, assuming licensing is a requirement of your local or state government (the license should be displayed at the mechanic's repair shop), and should have experience working on your particular type of car. If you don't already have a mechanic when your car breaks down and you need it fixed right away, you may end up taking it to a mechanic who charges too much or who does shoddy work.

Watch Out!

Don't work with a mechanic who tries to pressure you into paying for repairs that you do not understand or that you do not think your car really needs.

● Get problems with your car diagnosed and repaired as soon as you notice them. Prompt action helps ensure that small, relatively inexpensive problems don't grow into big, expensive ones.

● When practical, ride your bike, walk, or use public transportation to get to and from work. Carpooling with your coworkers is another option.

● If you own more than one car, sell the vehicles you don't really need. Keep the one that costs you the least to own and operate. If you have any money left over after you pay the loan balance on the car you sell, use it to pay off your highest interest debt and/or to build your savings.

● Trade in your current vehicle for one that is cheaper to own and to operate. Although paying for your gas-guzzling

SUV or zippy sports car may not have been difficult when you were financially flush, now that money is tighter, the vehicle may be putting a big strain on your budget. To find out which new and used vehicles are the most reliable and fuel efficient, go to Consumer Reports Online at *www. consumerreports.org* or read the most recent edition of *Consumer Reports Used Car Buying Guide.*

Money$ense

You will get the most money for your car if you sell it to an individual rather than to a dealer.

How to Get a Good Deal on a Used Car

You can get a great deal on a reliable used vehicle that meets your needs for a fraction of what you would spend for a new one if you take time to do up-front research into your used car options and to comparison shop. For example:

• Decide exactly what features you need in a car and how much you can afford to pay for a used vehicle. For example, if you do a lot of carpooling, buying a used station wagon or minivan makes sense, and if you live in a hot climate, you probably want a vehicle with good air-conditioning.

• Research your options. Use the *Consumer Reports* resources described above to find out about the vehicles that meet your needs and fit your budget. These resources will also provide you with information regarding a vehicle's original cost, safety record, and reliability.

• Familiarize yourself with the market value of the vehicles you are interested in so that you don't pay too much for them. The *NADA Official Used Car Guide* provides market value information. You can find the guide at your local library. You can also obtain this information by going to the Kelley Blue Book Web site at *www.kbb.com* or to Edmunds.com at *www.edmunds.com.*

• Purchase a used vehicle from a new car dealer who takes used cars on trade-ins or from an individual and avoid dealers that only sell used cars. Also, don't purchase a used car from an individual unless you are willing to have the car checked out thoroughly by a mechanic that you trust.

• When you find a car that fits the bill, examine its exterior in the daylight for dents, a poor paint job, or for other signs that it may have been in an accident. Also, test-drive the car in different driving situations, including stop-and-go traffic and on the highway. If you notice any problems, bring them to the attention of your mechanic.

• Review the car's repair records, examine its title to make sure that the seller actually owns the car, and ask the seller to provide you with a written statement of the number of miles on the car. Compare the statement to the number on the car's odometer. (If you are purchasing from a used car dealer, federal law says that the dealer must provide you with a written mileage disclosure statement.) If there is a difference between the two numbers, don't buy the car.

• Avoid cars with checkered pasts—vehicles that have been damaged by water, fire, or a wreck, and then rebuilt to look as good as new. To help ensure that you get what you think you are paying for, purchase a comprehensive history of the vehicle you want to buy from CarFax. Order the report by calling 888-422-7329, or by going to the CarFax Web site at *www.carfax.com*. Reports cost less if you order on-line. You can also provide your state motor vehicle department with the vehicle's 17-character Vehicle Registration Number (VIN) and ask it to run a title check on the car. (Most VINs are located on car dashboards, but some are on the inside of a car door or on its engine.) If the name on the title is different from the name of the person who is selling the vehicle, the vehicle may be stolen.

• Have your mechanic check out the vehicle you are interested in before you sign any sales paperwork or pay the seller any money.

• When you make an offer on the car, base it on the car's market value, not on the seller's asking price.

Spending Less on Food

Reducing the amount of money that your family spends on groceries each month can be easy, assuming you are willing to plan ahead and to use self-discipline. For example:

● Plan your meals for the coming week and then develop a shopping list around your meal plan. Take the list with you when you go to the grocery store so that you don't buy more groceries than you need.

● Read grocery store ads to find the best deals on the items on your shopping list.

● If money is really tight, shop with cash, not with your checkbook or debit card.

Money$ense

Go to ValuePage.com (*www.valuepage.com*) for coupons you can download and print on your computer. The site offers coupons for food, baby needs, bath and body care items, cleaning supplies, and more.

Money$ense

Bring a calculator with you when you shop at a warehouse, buying club, or discount house, since most of them don't provide unit pricing information.

● Use coupons. Yes, clipping coupons can be a hassle, but they can help you save as much as 25 percent on your purchases. Also, some stores offer clipless coupons, which are located on the shelf below a discounted item.

● Maintain a running list of staple items that regularly need to be replaced such as milk, paper towels, butter, bread, and so on. Post the list on your kitchen bulletin board, refrigerator, or somewhere else so that everyone in your household can add to it. The list will reduce the number of times you go to the grocery store each week. Fewer trips should mean lower grocery bills because the more often you shop, the more you tend to buy.

● Buy store or generic brands unless their quality is significantly inferior to the best-priced alternative name brands.

● Purchase items like laundry products, paper goods, body care items, cleaning supplies, and nonperishable food items that you use regularly at warehouse stores, buying clubs, or discount stores like Sam's, Costco, and Walmart. Resist buying items you don't really need or rarely use just because they are great deals. Also, don't buy jumbo-size perishable items like cooking oil unless you are sure that you will use them up before they spoil.

● Cook more meatless meals. Meals based on veggies, beans, and pasta are less expensive than meat-based meals—and healthier too.

● Avoid convenience items and prepared meals; they cost too much. If you don't want to spend a lot of time preparing meals at the end of each workday, on weekends cook and freeze casseroles, soup, stews and other easy-to-heat-up meals that you can eat the following week.

● Bring your own lunch to work. Make your children's school lunches too.

● Make dining out a treat, not a regular event. When you eat at home, you will spend less and you will probably eat less too.

● Enjoy your morning coffee at home before you leave for work or take it with you in an insulated mug rather than buying it at a coffee shop or carry-out restaurant.

Spending Less to Stay in Touch

With the advent of cell phones and the wide variety of optional extras like caller ID, voice mail, and call blocker that are now available, you probably spend a lot more to stay in touch by phone than you did just a few years ago. As a result it may not take much to reduce the size of your monthly phone bills. Furthermore, your reductions should have little or no impact on your family's standard of living. For phone-related savings:

● Reconsider your cell phone. Do you *really* need it? Probably not. For most people a cell phone is a convenience, not a necessity. If you truly believe that you can't do without yours, review your calling plan to make sure that it is appropriate given your usage and calling patterns. Your cell phone service provider should be willing to help you figure this out.

Money$ense

If another company offers you a better deal on your cell phone service, check to see when the contract on your current plan is up. If your contract is relatively new, the cost of canceling it may wipe out any savings you would realize by switching providers. If that is true, finish out the contract, but eliminate all optional extras.

● If you lease your cell phone, compare the cost of purchasing the same phone or a comparable phone. Owning is usually cheaper than leasing. By the way, you do not have to purchase your cell phone from the company that provides your phone service.

● Get back to basics with your home phone. Get rid of all nonessential extra lines and any of the "bells and whistles" you don't truly need. Month after month the cost of those extras can really add up. Same for your cell phone.

● Contact your long-distance provider to find out if you are eligible for a cheaper calling plan. Then shop around to see what other long-distance providers have to offer. A budget or flat rate plan may be appropriate depending on your phone usage.

● Limit your use of directory assistance.

● Write more letters, use E-mail more often, and make fewer long-distance calls.

Spending Less on Your Insurance

You need insurance in good financial times as well as bad. In fact, you need it even more when you are having money problems because that is when you can least afford to pay the cost of a claim out of your own pocket or not to be reimbursed for the kinds of expenses your insurance would cover. However, there are things that you can do to reduce the cost of your insurance coverage without significantly increasing your exposure to loss. Among other things you can:

● Ask your insurance agent to help you evaluate your insurance coverage and identify cost savings.

● Take advantage of any insurance discounts you may be eligible for. For example, you may be entitled to a discount if you do not use your car to get to and from work or if you purchase all of your insurance from one company. Also, if your home is in a disaster-prone area, you may be able to save money on your homeowners insurance by taking steps to disaster-proof your home. Talk with your insurance agent.

● Find out if you can purchase cheaper coverage by participating in any insurance programs that your professional association, civic group, or union may offer to its members.

● If your home has decreased in value, insure it for less. The value of your policy should reflect the replacement cost of your home and its contents, not your home's market value or property tax value, both of which reflect the value of the land your home is built on as well as the value of the structure itself and its contents. Depending on your neighborhood, the value of your land may be substantially greater than the value of your home.

● Increase the deductible on the collision and comprehensive portions of your auto insurance if you are driving an old vehicle that is not worth much. You may even want to drop the coverage for now.

● Consider asking your older children to find part-time jobs to help pay for their own insurance.

● Purchase a term life insurance policy if all you want is insurance protection, not the savings and investment products that come with other types of life insurance. If you want to purchase a whole life, universal life, or some other type of cash value policy, plan to hold it for at least 15 years. If you cancel one of these types of policies after just a few years, your life insurance costs can more than double.

● Convert your whole life insurance policy to a term life policy.

● Compare your current insurance coverage to the insurance programs you employer offers. You may be able to get comparable or even better coverage for less money through your employer.

● Talk with your employer's health plan administrator about ways to pay less on your medical insurance. In addition to increasing your deductible, you may be able to save by switching plans, from a PPO to an HMO for example. Another option is to enroll in a Flexible Spending Account (FSA) if your employer offers it. With an FSA you set aside a part of your salary, up to a certain amount, to pay for your family's health care. The income you allocate to your FSA will be tax free.

● If you lose your job, compare the cost of continuing your health insurance through COBRA to the cost of a temporary policy. Chapter 2 explains how COBRA works.

Spending Less to Dress

You can provide everyone in your family with plenty of attractive and up-to-date clothing items for a fraction of what you may be used to spending if you are willing to change where you shop and to plan ahead. For example, you can be a clothes horse on the cheap if you:

- Buy clothes when you need them, not for recreation.

- Identify items that need to be replaced because they have worn out and then purchase those items only.

- Purchase items at end-of-the-season sales when you know they will have to be replaced the next year.

- Resolve to buy all of your clothes on sale or to shop only at stores that sell items at mark-down prices like T.J. Maxx, Ross Dress for Less, and Marshalls.

- Shop at yard or tag sales. You can find some great deals at these sales. Bring cash.

- Make the clothes that you purchase for your younger children last longer by buying them just a little big.

- Swap clothes for yourself and your kids with your friends.

Spending Less on Yourself

When you are rolling in dough, you can afford to pamper yourself with body-care services, personal trainers, and so on. But when money is tight, it is time to give up those luxuries. For example:

- Give up manicures, pedicures, and massages, or view them as once-in-a-while special treats, depending on your money situation.

- Get your hair cut and colored less frequently.

- Evaluate the cost of your health club membership. Your local YMCA, YWCA, or community center may offer a less expensive alternative. However, if you are considering canceling your current club membership, check your membership agreement for any cancellation penalties. Take them into account when you are deciding whether to cancel it or to complete the membership and not renew it when it is up.

Watch Out!

Make sure that your health club membership does not renew automatically. To prevent the renewal, you may have to fill out a specific form and give it to the club a certain number of weeks prior to the end of your membership.

- If you are a smoker, kick the habit. If you need help, speak with your doctor. The Web site of The Foundation for a Smokefree America (*www.tobaccofree.org*) offers information about the dangers of smoking and tips for how to quit.

- Cut back on your drinking. If you and your spouse or partner enjoy a $20 bottle of wine each evening with dinner, you are spending nearly $8,000 a year on the fruit of the vine. If you believe that you may have a drinking problem and need help stopping, go to an Alcoholics Anonymous meeting in your area. Alcoholism is a progressive disease. If left untreated, your drinking problem will cost you more and more money, damage your health, and could even jeopardize your job and disrupt your relationships with the people you care about.

Spending Less on Prescription Drugs

Even with good health coverage, your out-of-pocket prescription drug costs can be substantial, especially if you or someone else in your family has a chronic health problem or a serious illness. That's the bad news. The good news is that there are ways to reduce your drug costs. For example:

- Purchase the generic equivalent of a prescription drug, assuming it will work just as well.

- Let your doctor know that you are having financial problems. She may give you free samples of the prescription drugs you need.

- Shop around for the best deal on prescription drugs by contacting drugstores in your area as well as grocery stores with pharmacies.

- Join the AARP if you are 50 or over so that you can use its mail-order discount pharmacy.

- Check out on-line pharmacies, including Phar-Mor (*www.phar-mor.com*), Rx Universe (*www.rxuniverse.com*), Pharmacy Sources (*www.pharmacysources.com*), Planet-Pills.com (*www.planetpills.com*), among many others.

Spending Less to Travel

The cost of travel seems to increase by leaps and bounds every year. However, savvy, budget-conscious travelers save money with planning and by taking advantage of insider tricks and know-how. You can do the same if you:

● Plan ahead to take advantage of advance-purchase airline tickets.

● When practical, you are flexible about the time of day you fly and the day you fly.

● Fly with low fare carriers.

● Rather than flying into and out of hub and big city airports, use alternative, less popular airports when possible.

● Use the Internet to shop for the best deal on your airline tickets. Visit travel Web sites such as Travelocity (*www.travelocity.com*) and Cheap Tickets (*www.cheaptickets.com*) to comparison shop. You can also use these sites to find deals on lodging, car rentals, cruises, vacation packages, and information about last minute deals. Also, don't overlook the airlines' own Web sites. They sometimes offer deals that are not available on the travel Web sites or that you won't find out about when you call the airlines to book a reservation.

● Purchase your airline tickets through a consolidator. A consolidator buys unsold tickets from airlines at big discounts and then sells them to individual travelers. If you work with a travel agent, find out if she works with a consolidator. You can also hook up with consolidators at About Network's budget travel site at *www.budgettravel.com.*

● Ask for the corporate rate, which is a discounted rate, when you book a hotel room or a rental car. Even if you are not traveling for business, you will get the rate if you ask for it. However, make sure that the corporate rate is the best deal you can get. You may get an even better deal if you are in the military, a senior, a member of an airline's frequent flyer club, or if you have booked a flight with a specific airline, et cetera. Don't wait for the reservation clerk to offer you a discount. Be proactive.

● Avoid calling a hotel chain's 800 reservation number when you want to book a room; call the specific hotel where you want to stay instead.

● Don't make long-distance phone calls from your hotel room. The hotel will probably charge you a fee or surcharge every time you do. By the way, if you are not given information about the surcharge or if there is no sign posted to inform you about the surcharge, you have the right to refuse to pay it when you check out.

● Try to avoid peak seasons when you are planning a vacation in a ski or beach resort.

> **Money$ense**
>
> About Network's budget travel Web site (*www.budgettravel.com*) provides how-to information and advice about staying in hostels, backpacking, using coupons and freebies, traveling as an air courier, working with a consolidator, and travel auctions as well as how to get a good deal on a hotel, a cruise, and so on. It also offers links to lots of travel-related Web sites. About Network is a great resource.

● Check to see what your auto insurance covers before you rent a car. The rental company will try to sell you a collision-damage waiver, but you don't need it if your own insurance provides that coverage. Also, you may have the coverage through your Visa, MasterCard, or American Express card.

4

MAKE MORE MONEY

When you don't have enough money to pay your bills or build up your savings, make more! You can increase your household income by working more hours at your current job, finding a new, better-paying job, changing careers, earning extra money on the side, or starting your own part-time business. This chapter tells you how to pursue each option and directs you toward resources that can help you achieve your money-making goals. It also explains how to choose a reputable vocational or career school if you need more education or training to increase your income, and it highlights federal student aid programs that can help you pay for it. The chapter also warns you about work-at-home scams and bogus business opportunities and advises you about what to do if one victimizes you.

Earn More Where You Work Now

If you don't want to change employers, here are suggestions for ways to increase your income where you are working now:

- If you are paid by the hour, ask to work extra hours. If your employer is having trouble meeting the demand for its product or services, is short-handed, or is expanding its operations, you may be able to work more hours by extending your workday, adding another shift to your schedule, or by working on weekends.

- Ask for a raise. Be prepared to justify your request for a salary increase. Possible justifications include:

  - Your on-the-job accomplishments.
  - The positive feedback you received during your most recent performance reviews.
  - The additional work responsibilities you have taken on without an increase in salary.
  - The fact that you have not received a raise in a long time.
  - The fact that you are being paid less than other employees in positions that are comparable to yours.

- Move up in the organization. If there is an opening for a better paying job that you believe you are qualified for, apply for it. Most companies like to promote from within.

If you don't get the raise or promotion that you wanted, find out why and what you can do to increase the chance that you can get one in the near future. If you are told that you need to improve your job performance, find out exactly where you fall short and ask when your performance on the job can be evaluated again.

Find a New Employer

No matter how much you think you may deserve an increase in salary, you may not get one if your employer is experiencing tough financial times or if your job skills or your role in the organization are not essential.

Look for a better paying job with a different employer if opportunities for a raise or promotion with your current employer

Money$ense

Consider on-line learning when you need more education to qualify for a promotion or to move into a new, more lucrative occupation. Online-Learning.net, which is owned by Sylvan Learning, is considered the leading on-line supplier of continuing higher education. It provides accredited, graduate-level extension courses in the areas of teacher education, business, and management, among other areas of study. The on-line classes are instructor led, but you can take them when it is convenient, from the comfort of your home or office. To review course listings, order a catalog, get cost information, and to obtain information on course instructors, go to www.onlinelearning.com.

are slim to none. To land a new job, you will need a well-written resume that succinctly describes your skills, experience, and professional accomplishments; a convincing cover letter; and solid interview skills.

If you want help preparing your resume, your state's public employment service or job service office may offer free assistance. If it cannot help you, the office may be able to refer you to organizations that can. If you can afford it, work with a resume services company or schedule an appointment with a career counseling firm. Among other services career counseling firms can help you market yourself effectively to potential employers. They are discussed later in this chapter.

Finding a new, well-paying job in today's market can be an uphill battle, especially if you live in an area where there are not many jobs in the first place. Therefore, don't get disheartened if you don't find a new job right away. It could take months to find a new one in this job market. To increase your chances of finding a new job sooner rather than later, take advantage of the job-finding resources that are described later in this chapter.

How to Find Out About Jobs You May Be Qualified For

When you are in the market for a new job, there are lots of ways to learn about positions you may be interested in. Here are some suggestions:

- Read the employment ads in your local newspapers and in newspapers in nearby communities. Some newspapers will e-mail you ads for jobs that match the kinds of positions you are looking for. Call your local paper to find out if this service is available, how to register for it, and how much it costs.

- Read the newsletter or magazine published by the trade or professional organization you belong to. Many of these publications include employment ads.

- Visit the Web site of the national office of the trade or professional organization you belong to. Some of these sites offer information about career opportunities.

• Tell your friends and family members that you are in the market for a new job and ask them to let you know if they hear of a position that may be right for you. The more people who know that you are in the market for a new job, the more apt you will be to hear about jobs that you are interested in.

• Let your former employers know that you want to change jobs, assuming you parted on good company. They may have the inside scoop on who is hiring. Do the same with your former coworkers, professional associates, and anyone else you can think of.

• Attend business networking events.

• Contact the job banks or job hotlines in your area. Many local, county, and state governments maintain information about job openings in both the public and private sectors. Call their human resource departments to find out if they maintain a job bank or a job hotline. Some professional organizations, trade associations and unions also have job banks. Call the ones you are interested in to find out. You may be able to access job bank information over the phone or via the Internet. Find out how often a job bank updates its job listings and contact it after each update.

• Get in touch with the human resources office of your local and county governments, if working for local government appeals to you. Personnel in these offices will tell you how to find out about job openings, advise you about the application process, and tell you about any tests you may have to take depending on the type of job you are interested in. They may also be able to provide you with information about other sources of job vacancy information and about local job-training resources.

● Schedule an appointment with your state's public employment service or job service office. These offices maintain information about public-sector job opportunities, including federal government jobs. Some of them also maintain information about for-profit and nonprofit job openings, offer free job counseling and referrals, conduct skills assessments, and provide resume development assistance.

● Find out about federal government jobs by visiting *www.usajobs.opm.gov* or by calling the United States Office of Personnel Management at 1-478-757-3000.

● Check with your local post office and visit the postal service Web site at *www.usps.gov* if you are interested in a job with the postal service. In many areas, the postal service also maintains a job hotline.

● Surf the Net. There are a wide variety of employment-related Web sites on the Internet so it may take some searching to find the right one for you. Here are some job search sites to start with:

- *www.ajb.dni.us* America's Job Bank lists more than 400,000 job openings and provides links to employment and training programs in every state.
- *www.careerbuilders.com* This comprehensive site claims to offer information about more than 300,000 positions. You can also use this site to have your resume distributed to recruiters on-line and to arrange to have information about jobs that you may qualify for sent to your E-mail

address. You can also access job search advice and counseling and learn about educational resources, including on-line resources, that can help you land the job you want.

- *www.careerjournal.com* This Web site is the place to go if you are in the market for a professional, managerial, or executive position. It is owned by *The Wall Street Journal*. In addition to job-opening information, the Web site features industry profiles; salary and hiring information; job-hunting advice; a calendar of free and low-cost career events, including job fairs; and articles about such topics as how to deal with sudden job loss, how to find a new job, and how to be a successful freelancer. Also, you can post your resume, or multiple resumes customized for different types of jobs, at this site, and if your experience and skills match a job opening, the job recruiter will send CareerJournal.com an E-mail. In turn, the Web site will forward the job information to you.

- *www.careerweb.com* This Web site features listings for a wide variety of jobs, from blue collar to white collar. You can also post your resume at this site and you can even do an on-line interview to get prequalified for a job that you are interested in.

- *www.hotjobs.com* This job site claims to be the number one jobs board. It features thousands of job openings that have been posted by corporate hiring managers, staffing firms, and executive recruiters.

- *www.jobs.com* In addition to a job search engine, this Web site features job postings and career development resources, including on-line resume assistance and job-search advice.

Money$ense

Use The Riley Guide at *riley-guide.com* to fine-tune your job search using the Internet. This site not only helps you figure out which Web sites will be the most helpful to you, but it also provides general advice and information about conducting a job search on-line.

- *www.monster.com* This Web site can help you locate a job in the health care, technology, retail, sales, human resources, legal, or financial fields. Its job listings range from administrative to senior executive positions. The site also offers resume help as well as information about salaries and industries. Use its sister site, *www.chiefmonster.com,* to search for high-level positions.

- Attend job fairs. Job fairs are a good way to find out which employers in your area are hiring and the kinds of jobs that they are trying to fill. You may even be able to do an initial interview for a position that interests you while you are at a job fair. Find out about job fairs in your area by reading the business section of your local newspaper. Learn about fairs around the country by going to *www.careerfairs. com.* For information about job fairs that specifically relate to high-tech and Internet jobs, visit *brassring.com.* This site features job listings as well.

- Contact companies you would like to work for to find out if they have any openings that you are qualified for. Even if the companies do not have any openings when you contact them, you may be able to get your foot in the door by sending your resume with a cover letter to the appropriate managers or to the companies' human resources departments. Follow up by telephone to make sure that your information was received. Later, when a job opens that matches your skills and experience, you may be asked to interview for it.

● Work with local employment agencies. If an employment agency specializes in your particular industry or occupation, contact it first. Before you agree to work with one, however, read the

Watch Out!

Steer clear of employment agencies that guarantee you a job. A legitimate agency will never make such a promise.

agency's contract. Make sure that you are clear about who will be responsible for paying the agency's fee if it finds you a job—you or the company that hires you. The fee is often a percentage of the salary you are offered. If it is your obligation to pay the fee, the contract should be clear about exactly how much you will have to pay and when the fee will be due.

● Schedule an appointment with an executive recruitment firm, or headhunter, when you are looking for a mid- to upper-level management or executive position. If the firm finds you a job, your new employer will pay the fee. Some of the firms you may want to contact are:

- Heidrick & Struggles International, *www.heidrick.com*. You can learn about the specific positions this executive search firm is trying to fill by going to *leadersonline.com*.
- Korn/Ferry International, *www.kornferry.com*. This company also maintains its own job site where you can search for available positions by job type. Go to *www.ekornferry.com*.

- Spencer Stuart, *www.spencerstuart.com*.
- TMP Worldwide, *www.chiefmonster.com*.

Career-Counseling Firms

The services of a career-counseling firm can be invaluable, especially in a tight job market. The firm can help you fine-tune your job search and can also help you ensure that you do an effective job of selling yourself to employers. Among other things, a career-counseling firm can help you:

- Assess your job skills and interests and advise you about any additional skills or knowledge you may need to land the job you want.

- Prepare an effective resume and cover letters.

- Hone your interview skills. Being prepared to respond to the kinds of questions you may be asked can make the difference between blowing an interview and putting your best foot forward.

> **Money$ense**
>
> The Business Women's Network at *www.bwni.com* and the Executive Women's Network at *www.ewn.com* offer career advice targeted to women.

- Target your job search.

- Negotiate job offers.

- Switch careers.

- Some career-counseling firms can help you negotiate a severance package with your current employer.

You may purchase a package of services for a fixed price from a career-counseling firm or you may be able to purchase the services you want on an à la carte basis.

Doctor, Lawyer, Tinker, Tailor? Deciding on a New Career

If you are working in a declining industry, or in an occupation where opportunities for advancement and growth are shrinking, you may need to change professions to make more money. Don't rush into a decision about what to do next. A career change is apt to have a profound affect on nearly every aspect of your life, for better or worse. Be sure that whatever new occupation you are considering offers opportunities for career advancement and growth, now and in the future. To help you decide what occupation to pursue:

• Think about the kinds of work you enjoy doing and about what you are good at. Also, think about what you do *not* want to do and are *not* good at.

• Find out which sectors of the economy and which occupations are projected to experience growth in the coming years. The U.S. Department of Labor's career information Web site, www.acinet.org/acinet, is a good source for this information. It tells you which occupations are the fastest growing, which have the most openings, and which ones pay the most. You can also research wages and trends for specific professions by state, link up with job and resume banks, job-search aids, occupational information and state resources, and you can search for sources of financial aid to help pay for the training or education you may need to change careers.

● *The Occupational Outlook Handbook* is a DOL publication that provides information on various careers by industry. It is updated every two years. Among other things, it describes the working conditions in various industries, the types of occupations that are available in each industry, the education and training needed to move into various occupations within different industries, and highlights opportunities for advancement by industry. It also provides earnings and benefits information for the industries it profiles, discusses the employment outlook for various occupations within those industries and features lists of other organizations that you can turn to for additional information. *The Occupational Outlook Handbook* is available on-line at *www.bls.gov/oco*.

● Research the employers in your area that are in high-growth industries and that hire people in the occupation you would like to move into.

● Figure out if you will need additional training or education to pursue the occupation.

Gear Up for a New Career by Attending a Trade or Vocational School

If you need education or training to make a career change, you can enroll in a college or university in your area on a part-time or full-time basis, or in a trade or vocational school. However, make sure that the school is reputable and has a good track record before you sign any paperwork or pay the school any money. Some schools are more interested in taking your money than in providing you with a quality education.

Take the following steps to check out a trade or vocational school before you enroll there:

- Ask for printed information about the school, the training you will receive, and the cost of the training, including tuition, books, lab fees, uniforms, equipment, and so on. If the school does not have printed information, don't enroll there.

- Request a copy of the school's contract so you can review it. Among other things, note whether you can cancel the contract, and, if you can, make sure that the contract spells out the process for getting your money back and indicates how long that process will take. If a representative of the school promises you anything that is not in the contract, ask that the promises be added to the contract, possibly as an addendum. If a school refuses to provide you with a sample contract or won't put its promises in writing, don't enroll there.

- Find out if the school has a job-placement program. If it does, find out what the school will do to help you find a job.

- Ask about the school's job-placement rate—the percentage of students who are placed in jobs relevant to their course of study—and about their average starting salary. If the school advertises its job-placement rates, it must also publish its most recent employment statistics, graduation statistics, and any other information necessary to back up its claims. This information must be available at or before the time that you apply for admission to the school.

● Request written information regarding the percentage of students who graduate from the program you want to attend. Avoid schools with high dropout rates.

● Find out about the qualifications and credentials of the school's faculty and how long the average instructor has been teaching there.

● Ask for the average number of students in the classes you will take.

● Sit in on some of the classes you will take so that you can observe the teaching styles of the instructors. Also, notice whether the classroom is clean and well maintained, whether the computers, tools, and equipment you will be trained on are state-of-the-art, and whether there are enough computers, equipment, and so on, so that everyone in the class has an adequate opportunity to use them.

● Talk with some of the students in the classes you observe to find out if they are happy with the school and feel that they are receiving a quality education. Also ask what they do not like about the school.

● Find out what financial aid may be available to you if you need help paying for your education. You may be eligible to participate in the federal education assistance programs offered through the U.S. Department of Education. Your state may offer education assistance too. When you speak with the school about financial assistance, the school should explain the pros and cons of government financial aid and make it clear that if you are approved for a student loan, you are legally obligated to repay the loan.

● Ask about the school's loan default rate—the percentage of students who attended the school, take out a government student loan, and then fail to repay their loans. A high default rate may mean that the school does a poor job of preparing students for

Watch Out!

Some accrediting organizations are phony. They exist to help make disreputable schools look reputable. If you have never heard of an accrediting organization, call your state department of education to make sure that it is legitimate.

the careers they want to pursue or that there are few job openings in those careers. Also, if the school you want to attend has a high default rate, you may not be eligible to participate in certain government financial aid programs.

● Find out if the school is accredited and/or licensed. If it is, get the name and phone number of the accrediting or licensing agency and contact them to confirm that the school's information is accurate. To be licensed or accredited, the school must meet certain minimum standards.

● Call some of the employers you would like to work for after you graduate from the school. Ask them if they would be more likely to hire you if you completed the program you are thinking about enrolling in.

● Make sure that there is not a less expensive way to get the training you want. For example, you may be able to get the same education for a lower price at your local community college. Also, don't overlook the possibility of on-the-job training.

● Check with your state attorney general's office of consumer protection, your local Better Business Bureau, and the Federal Trade Commission (FTC) to find out if any of them have complaints on file about the school. Avoid schools with a record of complaints. To contact the FTC, call 1-877-382-4357 or go to its Web site at *www.ftc.gov*. You can also write to the commission at: Federal Trade Commission, Consumer Response Center, 600 Pennsylvania Avenue, NW, Washington, D.C. 20580.

If you believe that a trade or vocational school has ripped you off, file a complaint against the school with your state attorney general's office of consumer protection, your local Better Business Bureau, and with the FTC. To file a complaint with the FTC, call 1-877-382-4357, use the on-line complaint form you will find at *www.ftc.gov,* or write to the FTC at the address provided in the last bullet. You may also want to consult with a consumer law attorney to discuss whether you have grounds for a lawsuit against the school.

Financing Your Education

The U.S. Department of Education (DOE) offers a variety of financial aid programs, including grants, work-study programs, and loans that can help you pay for the cost of your education and training. The educational assistance may be available to you regardless of whether you plan on attending a college, a university, or a trade or vocational school. DOE's financial assistance programs will help cover the cost of your tuition, books, and other fees.

The rest of this section provides an overview of many of the DOE financial assistance programs. For comprehensive information, read *The Student Guide,* which describes all of the DOE's financial aid programs as well as the application process for each program. To order a copy of *The Student Guide,* call the DOE's Federal Student Aid Information Center at 1-800-4-FED-AID (1-800-433-3243) or read an on-line version of the publication at *www.ed.gov.*

Once you decide on the federal student aid assistance you would like to apply for, you can fill out an on-line application by going to *www.fafsa.ed.gov.* You can also request a printed application from the DOE by calling 1-800-433-3243 or by writing: Federal Student Aid Information Center, PO Box 84, Washington, D.C. 20044.

Your state may offer its own education assistance programs. Get in touch with your state department of education or speak with the financial aid office at the school you want to attend to find out about the other assistance that may be available, including nongovernmental sources of financial aid. For the phone number of your state department of education, go to *www.ed.gov.*

Federal Pell Grants

You can apply for a Pell grant if you have not already earned a bachelor's or a professional degree. (According to the federal government, a professional degree is usually earned after a bachelor's degree in a field such as medicine, law, or dentistry.) You do not have to repay a grant.

If you receive a Pell grant, the size of the grant will depend on your financial need, the cost of the school you want to attend, and whether you enroll as a full-time or a part-time student, among other things. The federal government sets a ceiling on the maximum size of a Pell grant based on the level of Pell grant funding for an award year. During the 2002–2003 award year, the maximum Pell grant was $4,000.

When you are awarded a Pell grant, you may not receive the grant money directly. Instead the school you are attending may get the money and then apply it toward your school costs, or you may receive some and the school may receive some too. The school is obligated to send you a written notice telling you the size of your Pell grant, when the money will be released, and exactly who will receive the grant money.

Money$ense

The interest that you pay on your student loan may be tax deductible. Also, you may be eligible for a federal income tax credit. For example, the Hope tax credit is available to first- and second-year students who are enrolled in school at least half-time. It is worth up to $1,500 per student. Another tax credit, the Lifetime Learning tax credit, is equal to 20 percent of a family's tuition expenses, up to $5,000, for virtually any post-secondary education and training. You may be eligible for this tax credit even if you are attending school less than half-time. For more information on the Hope and Lifetime Learning tax credits, and other tax benefits for post-secondary students, visit www.ed.gov or read the IRS Publication 970. You can get a copy of this publication by calling 1-800-829-3676 or you can download it at www.irs.gov.

Stafford Loans

Stafford loans are a major source of financial aid for students. Depending on the school you attend, if you are approved for a Stafford loan, your loan will either be made through the Direct Loan Program or the Federal Family Education Loan (FFEL) Program. Both programs have the same eligibility requirements and loan limits. The major difference between the two programs is where the loan funds come from and your loan repayment options.

If you participate in the Direct Loan Program, your loan money will come directly from the DOE. However, if you are in the FFEL program, the money will come from a bank, credit union, or some private lender.

Depending on your financial status, your Stafford loan will be subsidized or unsubsidized. Subsidized loans are for individuals with a financial need. You will have to pay a four-percent fee for the loan regardless of which type of Stafford loan you have. The fee will be deducted proportionately from each loan disbursement. Also, if you don't make your loan payments on time, you may be charged late fees and collection costs.

Once you graduate, leave school, or drop below half-time enrollment, you will have a six-month grace period before you must begin repaying your loan. During this time if you have a subsidized loan, no interest will be charged. However, you will be charged interest if your loan is unsubsidized. In that case, you can either pay the interest as it comes due or it can be capitalized, which means that the total amount of your interest debt will be considered when the amount of your monthly loan payments is calculated.

Campus-Based DOE Aid Programs

The federal Supplemental Educational Opportunity Grant (FSEOG), the federal Work-Study (FWS) program, and the federal Perkins Loan program are labeled campus-based programs because they are directly administered by the financial aid office of participating schools. Schools may participate in some but not all of these programs. Each school sets its own deadlines for applying for campus-based funds. If you don't apply early for these funds you may be out of luck, because every year the DOE gives each participating school a certain amount of funds for its campus-based programs, and when a school uses up its allocation, that's it for the year.

If you apply for assistance from a campus-based aid program, the amount of aid you receive will depend on your financial need, how much other aid you are receiving, and on the availability of funds at the school you want to attend.

Here are brief descriptions of each program:

● *Federal Supplemental Educational Opportunity Grants* are available to undergraduates who have not earned a bachelor's or a professional degree and who have an exceptional financial need. If you qualify for a FSEOG, you will receive up to $4,000 a year.

● *The federal Work-Study program* provides part-time jobs for financially needy undergraduate and graduate students to help them pay their education expenses. The program focuses on finding students community service work or work related to their course of study. If you participate in this program, you will be paid by the hour for your work at a rate that is no less than the current federal minimum wage.

● *A Perkins loan* is a low interest loan—five percent. Undergraduate and graduate students with exceptional financial need are eligible for a Perkins loan. Undergraduates can borrow up to $4,000 for each year they are in school, but no more than $20,000. Graduate students can borrow up to $6,000 each year that they are in graduate school, up to $40,000. There are no fees associated with this loan but if you miss a loan payment or pay less than you are supposed to, you will be charged a late fee. You may also have to pay collection costs if you make a habit of paying late.

If you're attending school at least half-time, you will have a nine-month grace period after you graduate, leave school, or begin attending school less than half-time before you have to begin repaying the loan. At the end of the grace period, you may have up to ten years to repay your loan. If you're attending school less than half-time, speak with your school's financial aid office regarding how long your grace period will be.

Making Extra Money on the Side

You can make extra money by working at a second job, working as an independent contractor, or by starting a part-time business. If you want a second job, use the resources in the Change Employers section of this chapter to find one.

Many employers use independent contractors to augment their in-house expertise, to help them meet demand during a busy time of year—Christmas for example—or to reduce their costs without sacrificing quality. Writers, graphic designers, photographers, consultants, and other professionals often work as independent contractors. To find this kind of work, contact your professional associates, former employers, send marketing letters, brochures, and/or samples of your work to businesses that you believe may be interested in your services, and so on. You can also register at Web sites like *www.guru.com* that provide online opportunities for independent contractors to hook up with businesses and organizations around the country that may want to use their services.

If a business wants to work with you, your relationship will not be that of employer-employee, therefore, you will not receive paychecks or benefits from the business. Instead, you will provide the business an agreed upon service or set of services at a price you both agree on and you will have to invoice the business to get paid. The business will not deduct taxes from the money that it pays to you, but it will provide you with an IRS Form 1099 for income tax purposes. Be sure to use a contract or letter of understanding to spell out all of the terms and conditions of your business relationship.

Start a Part-time Business

Starting your own part-time business may seem like the solution to your money worries—once you become the next Bill Gates or Donald Trump, you can pay off your debts and you will still have plenty of money left to live on. The truth is however, it takes a lot of hard work to begin a business and to turn it into a success. In fact, statistics show that most small businesses fail and that those that do succeed often need an influx of cash during their early years to stay afloat. Therefore, your business could be a drain on your finances, not a cash cow.

To beat the odds, take some business-management classes before you plunge ahead with your business idea. Your local college or university may offer these classes on weekends or in the evenings. Also, check with your local chamber of commerce to find out if it sponsors business-management seminars for aspiring entrepreneurs. In addition there are many books on the market that cover the ins and outs of starting and running a successful small business. The resources section in the appendix to this book tells you about some of them.

After you take some business-management classes, you may conclude that self-employment is not for you. But if you decide that you are up to the challenge, the classes will give you a head start on business success.

Don't overlook the federal Small Business Administration (SBA) when you are setting up a part-time business. It can be a great resource every step of the way. The SBA offers technical and management assistance to start-ups as well as to established businesses, and it is the nation's single largest financial backer of small businesses. Among other things, the SBA publishes how-to brochures, runs an on-line business classroom and offers an on-line small business start-up kit. The kit walks you through every aspect of the business start-up process, provides information about financing your business, and includes an outline of a sample business plan that can help you prepare your own plan. The SBA's Web site is located at *www.sba.gov*. From there, you can link up with the SBA counseling center in your area and with other small business resources. You can also call the SBA at 1-800-827-5722 to speak with an SBA representative.

The Service Corps of Retired Executives (SCORE) is another small business resource you should know about. SCORE is a nonprofit organization dedicated to educating entrepreneurs and to helping them develop and grow small businesses. Working and retired executives and business owners donate their time and expertise as SCORE volunteer business counselors and provide confidential counseling and mentoring free of charge. For a full understanding of how SCORE can help you, and to locate the SCORE chapter nearest you, visit its Web site at *www.score.org*.

Beware of Bogus Business Schemes

If you are in love with the idea of owning your own business but you not sure what kind of business to start, you may be attracted by ads offering you the opportunity to earn big bucks as your own boss, regardless of your experience. These ads are everywhere—on TV, in newspapers, on the Internet, and on flyers posted on telephone poles at busy intersections. Some marketers go to great expense to make the business opportunities that they are selling appear legitimate. For example, some of them produce elaborate television programs, which usually air very early in the morning or late at night. However, the programs are actually *infomercials,* which are nothing more than very long advertisements—often as long as 30 minutes.

Although many business opportunities are legitimate—the opportunity to become part of a successful and well-established franchise for example—many of them are bogus. So, once again, before you spend any money or sign any paperwork related to a business opportunity, carefully check out the opportunity as well as the company that is marketing it.

According to the FTC's Franchise Rule, any company that markets a business opportunity must provide you with a "Franchise Disclosure Statement" at least ten days before you sign an agreement with the business or pay it any money. (Most business opportunities fit the FTC's definition of a franchise.) If you are not offered this statement, ask for one. If the business refuses to provide it, ask why. If the business tells you that it does not have to comply with the Franchise Rule, confirm this information by calling the FTC at 1-877-382-4357.

Even if the business is not legally obligated to provide you with a Franchise Disclosure Statement, for your own protection ask for it anyway. Any legitimate business will be happy to comply.

A Franchise Disclosure Statement provides the following information:

- The names, addresses, and phone numbers of previous purchasers. Contact some of them to find out about their experience as business owners. Better yet, visit them in person.

- The seller's fully audited financial statement.

- The cost of beginning and running the business opportunity.

- Your responsibility to the seller if you purchase the opportunity and the seller's responsibility to you.

- Any lawsuits that have been brought against the seller or its directors by previous purchasers as well as any lawsuits alleging fraud.

- The amount of any fees you must pay and under what conditions you can get them refunded.

• The number and percent of other purchasers who have earned at least as much as the seller claims you can earn.

Don't forget to check out a company that is marketing a business opportunity with your local Better Business Bureau, with your state attorney general's consumer protection office, and with the FTC. If the company contacted you via the mail, you should also contact the postmaster in your area because the post office investigates fraudulent mail practices. In addition, if the business opportunity requires a considerable financial investment, ask a business law attorney to review the information in its Franchise Disclosure Statement before you decide whether or not to invest in it.

If you are victimized by a bogus business opportunity, call the company that ripped you off and ask for your money back. Let the company know that you intend to report it to local law enforcement officials as well as the appropriate government agencies and offices, including the consumer protection department of your state attorney general's office, your local Better Business Bureau, and the FTC. If you get your money back, report the business anyway so that you can help protect other consumers from getting taken by it.

Maintain records of all your phone conversations and keep copies of any correspondence you send or receive related to this matter. Send your letters certified mail, return receipt requested. If you end up in court, the records may be helpful.

Work-at-Home Opportunities May Not Be What They Seem

When you are exploring ways to make extra money on the side, be wary of work-at-home opportunities. They may be advertised in your local newspaper, on a flyer or poster, in a recorded phone message, or a telemarketer may call to tell you about an opportunity.

Many work-at-home opportunities are not what they appear to be. For example, you may have to pay a substantial amount of money up front to purchase equipment or supplies to take advantage of an opportunity. In exchange the company that is marketing the opportunity may promise to provide you with software, manuals, technical support, or training. More often than not, however, you will either not get what you are promised or what you do get will be of very poor quality. Furthermore, you may never recoup your investment much less earn anything close to the amount of money you were promised.

Before you invest any time or money in a work-at-home opportunity, ask the company that is marketing the opportunity to provide you with printed information about itself and about the opportunity. Steer clear of any business that cannot provide you with printed information or that refuses to send any information until you pay it money up front.

If you do receive printed information, it should tell you, among other things:

- The company's address and phone number as well as information on the company's history.

- Your responsibilities and the company's obligations to

you if you invest in the opportunity. This information should be specific, not general.

● Exactly what you will receive for your investment.

● How you will be paid, who will pay you, how often will you be paid, and when will you receive your first check.

● The total cost of the work-at-home opportunity, including the cost of any supplies or equipment you may have to purchase.

The company marketing the work-at-home opportunity should formalize your relationship with a written contract that spells out all of its terms and conditions. Don't work with a company that does not use contracts, and don't pay it any money until you have received the contract and gotten answers to any questions you may have about it.

Before you sign the contract, check out the company with the consumer protection office of your state attorney general, your local Better Business Bureau, and with the Federal Trade Commission. However, many companies that are in the business of marketing bogus work-at-home opportunities regularly change their names and addresses so that they can avoid legal prosecution and continue making money by ripping off unsuspecting consumers.

You should contact these same offices if you are the victim of a work-at-home scam. You may also want to talk with a consumer law attorney to find out if you have any legal recourse. If you have a strong case, the attorney may take your case on a contingent-fee basis. With this arrangement the attorney takes her fee out of the money she wins for you. Typically the attorney will take between 30 and 50 percent. If the attorney loses your lawsuit, your attorney will not be compensated for her time and effort representing you. Win or lose, however, your attorney agreement may obligate you to pay for your attorney's expenses and court costs.

SOS

5

DIG YOURSELF OUT
OF DEBT

This chapter offers get-out-of-debt strategies that can help you reduce the amount that you pay on your debts each month and pay off your debts faster. Among other things the chapter explains how to negotiate more affordable debt payment plans with your creditors, how to transfer high-interest credit card debt to a lower interest card, and it reviews the pros and cons of your debt consolidation options. It also explains how debt-counseling firms and agencies can help you deal with your debts and tells how to find a reputable organization to work with. The chapter also warns you about get-out-of-debt scams, explains your legal rights when you are contacted by a debt collector, and provides invaluable advice about how to deal with your

Watch Out!

None of the get-out-of-debt strategies in this chapter are worth pursuing if you are not 100-percent committed to living within your means. Otherwise, once you get out of debt you are apt to get back into debt again, and you may end up in the same situation that you are in now.

past-due child support, student loans, and the federal taxes you owe but cannot afford to pay.

Negotiate with Your Creditors

When you are having trouble paying what you owe, contact your creditors to find out if they will negotiate new debt-payment plans with you that will reduce your monthly payments to amounts that you can afford to pay. If you believe that your financial problems will be short-lived, you may want to ask for your payments to be reduced temporarily, or you may want to propose making interest-only payments for a while. Otherwise, ask for a permanent change in your debt-payment agreement.

The sooner you contact your creditors, the better. Ideally you should contact them before you fall behind on your debts. If you wait too long, your creditors may be in no mood to help you out.

Before you contact your creditors, make a list of all of your debts, including the name of each creditor, the total amount of money that you owe to each creditor, your monthly payment for each debt, and whether a debt is secured or unsecured. When a debt is secured, list the asset that collateralizes it. This list will help you ensure that you do not overlook a debt and will help you identify the debts that you should focus on first. Remember, with a few exceptions, including past-due child support, money owed to the IRS, and a past-due student loan, secured debts are more impor-

Watch Out!

Depending on your state and on your loan agreement, if you get behind just one month on your car payments, the lender may have the right to take back your car with little or no prior notice. Chapter 6 explains how repossessions work.

tant than unsecured debts. (Chapter 2 explains the difference between a secured and an unsecured debt.) Below is a sample form
you can use to record your debt information.

DEBT INFORMATION SHEET

Name of Creditor / Total Amount Owed / Monthly Payment / Secured or Unsecured / Collateral

_____

_____

_____

_____

_____

_____

_____

_____

_____

Once you have recorded all of your debt information, review
your household budget to figure out how much you can afford
to pay on each debt. Be realistic! Then contact your creditors by
scheduling face-to-face meetings, calling them, or writing them
each a letter. If you contact your creditors by telephone, call their
customer service office, the office of their credit managers, or

Money$ense

Use the calculator at *www.bankrate.com* to figure out how long it will take you to pay off your debts based on how much you owe and how much you can afford to pay on them.

your loan officer. Exactly who to call depends on the creditor you are contacting. If you write to your creditors, model your letter after the example provided, although exactly what you should write will depend on your particular situation.

SAMPLE CREDITOR LETTER

Date

Your address

The creditor's address

Dear Sir or Madam:

I am writing you about my account, #_____. Presently I am experiencing financial difficulties because _____. Therefore, I am having problems making the monthly payments that I owe to you. However, I have taken the following steps to take control of my financial situation. I have (Explain what you have done. For example, you have reduced your living expenses, set up a household budget, taken a second job, moved into a less expensive place to live, and so on).

As part of this effort I am contacting my creditors to explore the possibility of negotiating lower monthly payments on my credit accounts. I am anxious to meet my debt obligations and paying less each month will help me do that.

Presently I owe a total of $_____ on my account with you

and my monthly payment is $_____. I would like to begin paying $_____ a month instead at the same rate of interest that I pay now. (You can also propose an interest reduction or that you will make interest-only payments for a specified period of time.)

I believe that this is a fair and realistic request since my current monthly net household income is $_____ and I have only $____ left over each month after I pay all of my living expenses. I would like an opportunity to discuss this matter with you by telephone as soon as possible. I can be reached during working hours at (your daytime phone number including area code).

Thank you for your consideration.

Best Regards,

Your Signature (as it appears on the credit account)

However you contact your creditors, tell them why you are having financial problems—a job loss, a sudden illness, poor money-management skills, a divorce, and so on—and reassure them that you want to pay what you owe, but let them know that you need a more affordable debt repayment plan to do that. Be sure to explain what you have done to improve your financial situation—you took a second job, you set up a household budget, you stopped using credit, you enrolled in a money-management class, et cetera. Also, if any of your creditors ask, be prepared to tell them the total amount of debt that you owe, the total amount of your net monthly income, and the total amount of your living expenses (rent or mortgage, food, utilities, phone, child care, et cetera) as well as the total value of your assets.

When you are figuring out how much you can afford to pay to your creditors, it's a good strategy to come up with two amounts—a lower amount and a slightly higher, but still afford-able amount. If your creditor thinks the lower amount is too little, you can keep the negotiations going by offering to pay the higher amount.

During your negotiations, try to remain calm and never be rude or demanding. If you feel yourself getting upset, end the conversation and call back later once you have your emotions back under control. If the first person you speak with does not have the authority to help you or won't work with you, ask to speak with her manager.

Stick to your guns if a creditor tries to pressure you into paying more than you think you can afford. The risk of agreeing to pay too much is that you won't be able to keep up with the payments. If you fall behind, the creditor may not be interested in giving you a second chance. Instead it may send your account to collections or sue you to take back its collateral. As a result you may have to file for bankruptcy.

Keep a record of your conversations with your creditors, including the dates of each conversation, the name of the person you spoke with, and the upshot of the conversation. File your notes in a safe place so that you can refer to them later if necessary.

If you reach an agreement with a creditor, write down the terms of the agreement and then put them in a letter. Make a copy of the letter for your files and send the original to the person you spoke with. Send it certified mail, return receipt requested. File the receipt as well.

Leave the Negotiating to Someone Else

Schedule an appointment with the Consumer Credit Counseling Services (CCCS) office in your area if you want someone else to negotiate with your creditors. The CCCS is part of the nonprofit National Foundation for Consumer Credit, which is the nation's largest credit counseling network. It offers low-cost/no-cost assistance to financially troubled consumers, including budgeting assistance, debt-payment negotiations, and money-management education. Creditors respect CCCS and may be more open to working with you when they know that you are a CCCS client. To locate the CCCS office nearest you, go to *www.nfcc.org,* or call 1-800-388-2227.

After reviewing all of your financial information, your debt counselor will either help you figure out a way to pay your debts according to your current agreements, or, if you owe too much, the counselor will try to negotiate new debt-payment agreements with your creditors. Assuming the counselor is successful, after all of the details of the new agreements are finalized you will begin sending payments for the creditors who are participating in the plan directly to your CCCS counselor, who in turn will pay your creditors. You will be charged a fee to set up your plan as well as a monthly maintenance fee.

If there is not a CCCS office near you, check with Credit Counseling Centers of America at 1-800-493-2222 (*www.cccamerica. org*) or with the Association of Independent Consumer Credit Counseling Agencies at 1-703-934-6118 (*www.aiccca.org*) to find out if either of these nonprofit debt-counseling organizations have an office in your area. You can also check your local Yellow Pages under *Credit and Debt Counseling, Debt, or Debt Adjusters* for other sources of debt-counseling assistance.

If there is not a debt-counseling organization in your area that belongs to one of the three networks mentioned here, carefully screen the organizations you are considering, because the debt-counseling industry is largely unregulated. Therefore, it is easy for disreputable firms and agencies to take advantage of unsuspecting consumers. For example, presently only seventeen states have laws that govern the activities of debt-counseling organizations and many disreputable organizations set themselves up as nonprofits because the Federal Trade Commission will have no authority over them.

How to Find a Reputable Debt-Counseling Organization

Most debt-counseling organizations are truly interested in helping consumers deal with their debts, but there are some bad apples. Therefore, before you pay money to one, or sign any paperwork, be sure to get answers to the following questions:

- What services do you offer?

- What educational programs do you offer? Better debt-counseling firms offer a variety of programs designed to help you become a better money manager, including classes on household budgeting.

- How do you charge for your services?

- Do I have to pay money up front and if I do, how much? Some firms will ask you to make an up-front payment of as much as a couple of hundred dollars. Don't pay any money until you are sure that the firm is on the up-and-up and until you fully understand what you will get for your money. Some disreputable debt-counseling firms will take your money and run.

● Do I have to pay any other fees? Watch out, a lot of small fees can add up over time.

● Do you use a written contract? Don't work with a debt-counseling firm that does not use a contract. The contract should spell out the specific services you will be provided along with their terms and conditions and the total cost of the services.

● Will I be assigned a specific counselor? This is the preferable arrangement.

● What kind of training, certification or accreditation, and experience do your counselors have? Some "counselors" are little more than telemarketers who are only interested in signing up as many clients as possible.

● Do I have to owe a minimum amount of debt to get your help?

● What can I expect if I work with you?

● How will you help me if I have problems meeting the terms of the debt repayment plan you negotiate for me?

● Will I send my debt payments to you or will I continue to send them directly to the creditors who participate in the debt-payment plan you negotiate for me? If I send them to you, how will I be notified each month that you have paid my creditors?

- How often will I receive written updates on the status of my debts? Can I access that information at your Web site or by calling a special number?

- How will you protect my personal and financial information? Make sure that the debt-counseling organization will not sell this information.

Avoid debt-counseling firms that do not have printed information about their services and fees, that refuse to mail their information to you if you ask for it over the telephone, or that tell you that they won't give you the information unless you answer some questions first. Also steer clear of firms that offer their services on-line or by phone and that automatically put you into a debt-repayment plan without first determining if you can pay your debts after appropriate financial counseling.

Before doing business with any debt-counseling firm contact your state attorney general's consumer protection office and your local Better Business Bureau. Find out if they have any complaints on file about the firm. You should also contact your state banking commission or department. In some states this department maintains records of complaints against debt-counseling agencies and firms.

Don't be fooled! Some debt-counseling firms choose names that make them sound like they are nonprofits. They hope that if you think they are a nonprofit, you will not check them out before you agree to work with them.

Consolidate Your Debts

Debt consolidation can be a good strategy when you have too much debt. Consolidating debt involves borrowing money to pay off all or some of your debts. If you cannot consolidate all of your debts, you may still come out ahead by consolidating some debts. Start with your highest interest debt. However, debt consolidation is not a good idea unless it allows you to:

- Lower the interest rate on your debts. The interest rate on the consolidated debt should be lower than the rates on the debts you pay off. A lower rate means that it will cost you less to get out of debt.

- Reduce the amount of money that you pay on your debts each month.

- Get out of debt faster. Ideally, you should be able to pay off the consolidated debt within five years, the maximum amount of time you would have to pay off most debts if you filed a reorganization bankruptcy. However, this rule of thumb does not apply to your mortgage loan.

- Reduce the number of debt payments you make each month. The fewer the payments, the fewer due dates you will have to juggle and the less likely you are to run up late fees.

You have a number of debt-consolidation options. For example, if you have a lot of high-interest credit card debt, you can transfer your card balances to a credit card with more attractive terms. You can also get a personal loan from a bank or credit union and use the proceeds to pay off your debts. Home

Money$ense

Use the "real cost of your debt" calculator at the Bankrate.com Web
site when you are shopping for a
loan to consolidate debt. The calculator can help you figure out how
much money you will pay over the
life of the loan based on the loan's
principle—the amount you are borrowing—the loan's interest rate and
the length of the loan.

equity loans, borrowing against your insurance policy or your 401(k) are other options as well. The most appropriate debt-consolidation method for you depends on the details of your financial situation and on the specifics of the method you are considering. Consult with a reputable debt counselor, with your banker, or with your financial advisor to be sure that the debt-consolidation method you are considering is the best one for you.

The next section of this chapter explains how various debt-consolidation methods work. However, when you are evaluating your options, keep this advice in mind

● Steer clear of consolidation offers that come with a lot of fees. The fees will dramatically increase the real cost of your borrowing. For example, a loan with a low interest rate and a lot of fees may end up costing more than a loan with a slightly higher rate but fewer fees or less expensive fees.

● Avoid a debt-consolidation loan that gives you extremely low payments spread out over many years. Although a low, low monthly payment may seem attractive, by the time you have paid off the debt, you may end up paying far more in interest than if you had just kept paying off each of the debts you consolidated. Also, if the loan is collateralized and you have to make a balloon or lump-sum payment at the end of the loan, if you cannot afford to make the payment, you could lose the asset that secures the debt.

● Don't trade unsecured debt for secured debt. As you learned in the previous chapter, there is not much that an unsecured creditor can do to hurt you when you cannot afford to pay the money that you owe. On the other hand, a secured creditor can take back your collateral.

● Avoid trading fixed-rate debt for variable-rate debt. A loan with a variable rate could end up costing you a bundle if the interest rate increases. For example, a loan may begin with a low, low teaser rate that lasts for just a couple of months but then jump—maybe to a rate that is higher than the rates on the debts you paid off with the loan. You may face the same problem if you transfer credit card balances to a credit card with a low introductory rate that goes up once the introductory period is up, or that increases as soon as you are late with an account payment.

Make a Transfer

Transferring high-interest credit card debt to a card with a lower rate is a good way to consolidate debt if:

● You are no longer using your credit cards.

● You are committed to paying more than the minimum due each month on the transferred debt. If you just pay the minimum, it will take years for you to pay off the debt and it will cost you hundreds of dollars in interest.

● The card's low rate is a fixed, not a teaser or "low intro-ductory rate." Although you can transfer the balance on the low-rate card just before the rate is due to increase, if you are not good at keeping track of such things, a fixed-rate card is better. Another option is to pay off the transferred balance before the low interest rate expires.

● You are sure that the lower interest rate applies to the balances you are transferring. Some companies promote low-rate credit cards but apply a higher rate to a transferred balance.

● The transfer fee is not excessive.

● You fully understand all of the terms and conditions of the balance transfer. For example, will the card's interest rate increase if you make a payment late? Will the new rate be higher than the rates on the credit card debt you transferred? Read the fine print!

To consolidate your credit card debt with a balance transfer, call the customer service number for the lowest rate credit card you have. Find out what terms and conditions the credit card company can offer you on a balance transfer. Be prepared to tell the person you speak with exactly how much debt you want to transfer. Then, using the credit card comparison criteria discussed in chapter 2, compare those terms and conditions with any balance-transfer offers you may have received in the mail. You can also shop for a more attractive offer by reviewing informa-tion about specific credit cards at CardWeb.com (*www.cardweb.com*) and at Bankrate.com (*www.bankrate.com*).

Get a Personal Loan

If your debt-to-income ratios are okay (chapter 2 highlights these ratios) and your credit record is still in relatively good shape, you may be able to consolidate your debt by getting an unsecured loan. If you cannot qualify for an unsecured loan, or if you want a loan with a lower interest rate, apply for a secured loan, assuming you have an asset that you can use as collateral such as a vehicle, the money in your savings account, a Certificate of Deposit, et cetera.

Contact your bank or credit union to find out what kind of loan it can offer you, but don't stop there. Check with other lenders to see if they can offer you a loan with better terms.

> **Money$ense**
>
> If you qualify for a secured or unsecured loan, find out if you can get a lower interest rate if your loan payments are automatically debited from your checking account each month.

Borrow from Someone You Know

A loan from a friend or family member may seem like the answer to your prayers, especially if a traditional lender will not give you a loan to consolidate your debts. After all, no application to fill out, no closing costs, no credit check, and maybe even no interest to pay. What more could you ask for?

Although borrowing money from someone you know is easy and inexpensive, if you don't keep up with your loan payments or if the lender decides to call the loan, your relationship with one another could be damaged or even destroyed. Therefore, don't even consider asking someone you know to loan you money unless:

● You are willing to be totally up front about the state of your finances. The person you want to borrow from is entitled to have this information before deciding whether or not to lend money to you.

● You are certain that you can afford to repay the loan.

● You are willing to treat the loan as seriously as you would treat a bank loan.

If your friend or family member agrees to lend you money, put the terms of the loan in a written agreement. Among other things, the agreement should state the amount of the loan, the duration of the loan, the interest rate on the loan (assuming you will be charged interest), when each of your loan payments will be due, when you will be considered late with a payment, and the amount of any late fee you may be charged. The agreement should also state when you will be in default of the loan and what will happen if you default. Once you have a loan agreement that you are both happy with, you and the lender should sign duplicate originals and you should each take one for your files. If there is only one original, the lender should take the signed original and you should get a copy.

If you are borrowing a substantial amount of money—a thousand dollars or more—make the lender a secured creditor by collateralizing the loan with one of your assets. Then, if you default on the loan, the lender can take the asset in payment. Also, if you file for bankruptcy, your friend or family member will be in a better position to get paid because secured creditors get paid before most other creditors in a bankruptcy. If you put up collateral, your loan agreement should describe the collateral and should state when the lender is entitled to take it. If you collateralize the loan by giving your friend or family member a lien on a vehicle you own, be sure to register the lien with your state's motor vehicle department. Model your agreement after the one below.

SAMPLE LOAN AGREEMENT

Date

In exchange for receiving a loan of $_____ from (lender's name), I, (your name), agree to repay the loan by making (number) equal payments in the amount of ($ amount of each loan payment) no later than (due date for loan payments) each month. If I am late with a payment, I agree to pay a late fee of ($ amount of late fee). The period of the loan will be from (date of first payment) to (date of last payment).

I am collateralizing the above described loan with (Describe the asset you are using as collateral, e.g. my 1998 Mazda Miata. The collateral should be approximately the same value as the amount of the loan). I understand that if I fail to make (number of missed payments after which you will be considered in default) payments in a row, (name of lender) has the right to take the collateral as payment.

Your Signature

Date

Borrow from Yourself

Borrowing the money from your life insurance policy, 401(k) or 403(b) are other debt consolidation options. However, although each of these assets represents a relatively quick and easy source of cash, borrowing from them to pay off your debts comes with some significant drawbacks. The following sections of this chapter explain how each of these borrowing options works and highlights their pros and cons.

Tap In to Your Retirement Funds

If your plan allows it, you can borrow up to one half the value of your 401(k) or 403(b) but no more than $50,000, at an interest rate that is a point or two above the prime rate. The prime rate changes from time to time. Call your bank, read the financial pages of your local newspaper, or go to *www.bankrate.com* to find out the current rate. You will have five years to pay back the money. You cannot borrow against your Individual Retirement Account (IRA).

If you decide to withdraw money from your 401(K) or 403(b) before you reach age 59½, the funds will be subject to income taxes and to a 10-percent early-withdrawal penalty. However, if you qualify for a "hardship withdrawal" because of an immediate financial need, you may be able to avoid the penalty, but not the tax liability. Money to prevent an eviction or foreclosure, to pay medical expenses, or to cover the costs of tuition, room and board, and fees for the next twelve months of a post-secondary education are examples of a financial need that might qualify for a hardship withdrawal. Talk with your plan administrator, CPA, or with some other financial advisor about early withdrawals.

If you borrow against your 401(k) or 403(b) account and

then you leave your job, your employer can require you to repay the full amount of the loan right away. If you don't and you are younger than 59½, the loan will be treated like an early withdrawal, which means that you will have to pay a penalty and that you will be taxed on the borrowed money. Therefore, if you are concerned about the loss of your job or if you are actively looking for a new one, borrowing from your retirement account is probably not a good idea.

Borrow Against Your Life Insurance Policy

Borrowing against the cash value of your whole life insurance policy

Watch Out!

When you borrow against your retirement account, the borrowed money will not earn interest. Therefore, the account will grow more slowly. If you are young and have many years of work ahead of you, this may not be a problem, but it could be an important drawback to this option if you are close to retirement age.

Watch Out!

When you have a cash value policy, the insurance company pays interest on the policy each year, but when you borrow against the policy, you will earn less interest. Therefore, the actual or effective rate on an insurance loan is higher than the rate stated in your policy.

is an attractive way to consolidate debt because the interest rate on the loan will be relatively low and because you do not have to repay the loan according to any set schedule. In fact you do not have to repay it at all. However, the amount that you do not repay will be deducted from your policy's total death benefit, and as a result the beneficiary of the policy will receive less money when you die. If the policy beneficiary is your spouse or partner and she is counting on the death benefit to help pay the bills once you are gone, a smaller benefit could make life difficult for her.

Before you borrow against the cash value of your insurance policy, read the policy to learn the terms and conditions of the loan. Also, talk with your insurance agent to be sure that you understand the true cost of the loan and the potential impact of the loan on your policy's death benefit.

Borrow on Margin

Generally, you can borrow up to 50 percent of the market value of your stocks and up to 90 percent of the value of the bonds you own, although the exact percentage depends on the type of bond and when it matures. The interest rate on a margin loan is usually just a few points above the prime rate, but since you will not be earning interest on the investments that you borrow against, the effective rate is higher. You do not have to pay off a margin loan according to a particular schedule or by a certain deadline.

As attractive as a margin loan may sound, it is not recommended for most investors, because if the value of the investment that you borrow against drops below a certain level, there will be a margin call and you will have to repay all, or most, of the loan immediately.

When you borrow on margin, plan on paying off the loan as quickly as you can to minimize the risk of a margin call. Although your investment portfolio may be making lots of money when you borrow on margin, as you have already seen from what happened to tech stocks not long ago, you cannot predict when the market will drop and the value of your holdings along with it. Paying off a margin loan right away is particularly important if you will be retiring soon and need every penny of your investments to fund your retirement.

Mine the Equity in Your Home

You may be sitting on a gold mine if you are a home owner and your home has appreciated a lot since you bought it. You can mine that gold to consolidate your debt by borrowing against your home's equity. Equity is the difference between the current value of your home and the amount of money that you still owe on it. Most lenders will let you borrow up to 80 percent of your equity and will give you between 5 and 15 years to pay off the loan. However, shoot for the shortest term loan you can afford and make sure that your loan payments are at least as much as the total of your monthly payments on all of the debts that you pay off with the loan proceeds.

Consolidating debt with a home equity loan offers some important advantages. They include:

● The loan application process is fast and simple. In fact, you may find out if you have been approved for a home equity loan the same day that you apply for it.

● It is easy to qualify for a home equity loan, assuming you have a good mortgage payment history and the rest of your finances are not a disaster.

● Home equity loans come with relatively low interest rates. Also, depending on how much you borrow, the interest on the loan will be tax deductible.

The main drawback to a home equity loan is that it is secured by your home. Therefore, if you don't keep up with the payments, you could lose the home.

Money$ense

A home equity line of credit is an alternative to a home equity loan. It lets you borrow against your equity as you need to, up to a stated dollar amount. Your home equity line of credit will come with a variable interest rate, and your credit line payments will vary depending on how much of the credit line you use and on the prevailing interest rate. Like a home equity loan, your home will secure the line of credit and therefore, the line of credit has the same drawbacks as a home equity loan.

Another important drawback to a home equity loan is that if your home's value drops after you have the loan, the amount of money you owe on it (the balance on your home mortgage plus the balance on the home equity loan) could exceed what your home is worth. Therefore, if you were to sell it, you would have to make up the difference between what it sells for and what you still owe on it. In fact, the new owner cannot take title to the home until you do.

If you want to consolidate your debts using a home equity loan, shop around for the best deal. Federal law requires home equity lenders to give you specific information regarding the terms and conditions of their loans when they provide you with a loan application. You may also be able to get this information over the telephone.

When you compare the costs of your home equity loan options, consider the size of the application fee and any other loan-related fees and expenses you may have to pay. Other expenses may include: the cost of a survey, an appraisal, and title insurance, as well as attorney fees, recording fees, and points. (A point is prepaid interest and it is equal to one percent of a loan's value. The number of points you are asked to pay will vary from lender to lender. You may be able to negotiate the number of points you have to pay.) Don't hesitate to ask each of the lenders you contact if they will lower or even waive some of their fees and expenses. Also, make sure that you can get your application fee back if you are turned down for a loan.

Pay close attention to the loans' terms and conditions. For example, some loans begin with a low introductory interest rate, but after several years the rate increases substantially. When you are considering a loan like this, don't focus on the low introductory rate unless you are confident that you will pay off the loan balance before the introductory rate is up. Instead, make sure that you can afford the payments once the higher rate kicks in.

Before you sign any loan paperwork or pay any fees, it's a good idea to ask someone you trust—your financial advisor, a nonprofit debt counselor, your CPA, even a financially savvy friend—to review all of the information you have about the loan, including the loan agreement you will have to sign. That person may find problems with the loan that you did not notice because you were so anxious to get out of debt. Remember, it pays to be extra careful when you are applying for a loan that is secured by your home.

Watch Out!

Some unscrupulous lenders prey on home owners who are looking for a way out of their money troubles. For example, they may encourage you to overstate your income on your loan application so you can qualify for a home equity loan that you cannot really afford. They are gambling that you will fall behind on your loan payments. If their gamble pays off, you will lose not just the roof over your head but all of the equity you have in your home as well. If you believe that an unscrupulous lender has victimized you, get in touch with a consumer law attorney right away. Chapter 5 provides you with resources for finding a good consumer law attorney.

Refinance Your Mortgage and Get Cash Out

If mortgage rates have dropped since you got your home loan, refinancing the loan and adding enough money to the new loan to pay off your debts may make sense. However, depending on the costs involved, the length of the new loan, the rate on the new loan, and on how much equity you have in your home, refinancing to consolidate debt may not be a smart move. Therefore, don't refinance without getting outside advice from someone you trust such as your nonprofit debt counselor, financial advisor, banker, et cetera. Also, this option and home equity loans share the same danger. If you fall behind on your payments, you could lose your home.

Watch Out!

Before you refinance, make sure that your current mortgage agreement does not have a prepayment penalty. If it does, take the size of that penalty into account when you are comparing the cost of refinancing to your other debt-consolidation options.

If you do refinance, federal law says that the lender must give you three days to cancel the loan after you have signed all of the loan paperwork. This *right of rescission* applies to any kind of loan that you secure with your home, including a home equity loan. To cancel the loan, fill out the cancellation form that you should have received from the lender.

Don't Even Consider These Debt Consolidation Offers!

When you are anxious to get out of debt, you may be tempted by get-out-of-debt offers that sound too good to resist. However, there are plenty of companies ready to prey on people in your financial situation, so check all of their get-out-of-debt offers. Many of them will make your financial situation worse, not better. Debt-consolidation offers to avoid include:

● Finance company loans. These loans usually come with a high rate of interest and with more fees and expenses than bank and credit union loans. For example, finance companies often charge steep application fees and high closing costs for their loans. Also, having a finance company loan on your credit record will damage your credit record.

● Loans made by debt-counseling organizations. Some shady debt-counseling organizations make high interest loans to their clients. They may also require that their clients collateralize the loans with their homes.

● Advance fee or guaranteed loans. Businesses that make these kinds of loans often advertise that you can get a loan regardless of the state of your finances and the condition of your credit record. Many of them require that you pay an up-front fee of between one and several hundred dollars, or even more. A reputable lender will never promise to loan you money until it has reviewed your financial information and your credit record, nor will it ever demand money from you until after you have completed a loan application. Not only are advance-fee loans very expensive, but some advance-fee

> **Watch Out!**
>
> Some finance companies make it seem like they are giving you a debt-consolidation loan, but in fact you are getting a home equity loan. Never collateralize a finance company loan with your home.

companies will disappear as soon as they get your up-front payment.

● Loans from bill-paying companies. These companies may make it sound like they are giving you a debt-consolidation loan, but what they are really doing is paying your bills each month, for a fee. Furthermore, you will have no recourse if they do not pay your bills on time, and the bill-paying company may even disappear with your money. Some deal!

How Not to Get Taken

Disreputable companies prey on financially troubled consumers who are desperate to improve their situation. Follow this advice to avoid becoming one of their victims:

● Do not sign a loan agreement without reading it carefully, line by line. Ask questions about anything you do not understand. If you are not sure that a company is on the up-and-up, let it know that you want someone else to review the agreement. Then, ask a consumer law attorney, your debt counselor, CPA, or someone else you trust to read it. Don't work with a company that refuses to let you leave with the loan agreement.

● Never pay money up front to guarantee a loan.

● Be extra careful if you are asked to use your home as collateral.

● Avoid businesses that advertise that they work with consumers who have bad credit.

• Be skeptical of any company that approaches you about a loan, especially if the company is not a respected bank or credit union in your community.

• Check out the lender with your state's banking authority and the consumer protection office of your state attorney general's office. Find out if these offices have any complaints on file about the business, but bear in mind that a lack of complaints does not always mean that the business is reputable. Some disreputable businesses make a habit of changing their names to stay one step ahead of the law. Contact the FTC and your local Better Business Bureau too.

If You Get Ripped Off

If you believe that you have been ripped off by a company that promised to help you consolidate your debts—you were misled about the terms of the loan, you paid a fee but never received the loan you were promised, and so on—contact the company and demand your money back. Although it's a long shot, especially since many unscrupulous businesses regularly change their names and addresses to avoid being caught, it is worth a try.

If you do locate the company, tell the business owner or manager that unless you get your money back, you will report the business to the office of your state attorney general, to your state's banking commission or department, and to the Federal Trade Commission (FTC). The business may try to avoid trouble by returning your money. However, follow through on your threat whether you get your money back or not. Chapter 4 explains how to file a complaint with the FTC.

None of those government offices will take action on your behalf. However, if they receive enough complaints about a particular business or about a particular business practice, they may act on behalf of all the consumers who were victimized. Also, by filing a complaint, you are helping to prevent other consumers from getting ripped off like you were.

Finally, consult with a consumer law attorney about whether you have grounds for a lawsuit against the company. If she believes that you have a strong case, she may represent you on a contingent-fee basis. Chapter 4 explains how contingent fees work.

Special Considerations Related to Special Kinds of Debts

Certain kinds of debts, including student loans, court-ordered child-support obligations and the income taxes you owe to Uncle Sam merit special attention. This section of chapter 5 explains what may happen if you do not pay these debts and reviews your options for dealing with each of them.

Federal Student Loans

When you can't afford to keep up with your federal student-loan obligations, you may be able to avoid defaulting on the loan by getting a loan deferment or forbearance. You may even be able to get your debt discharged or cancelled.

If you owe money on multiple Stafford loans, consolidating the loans into a single student loan may also be an option. You will apply to the Department of Education (DOE) if you have

Direct Stafford loans, but to the agency or lender that is holding your loans if you have a Federal Family Education Loan (FFEL) Stafford loan. You may be eligible for a debt-consolidation loan even if you have defaulted on one or more of your student loans. To learn more about consolidating your student loans, contact the DOE's loan-origination center consolidation department at 1-800-557-7392 or go to *www.loanconsolidation.ed.gov*. Chapter 4 explains Stafford loans.

A Stafford loan deferment temporarily postpones your loan payments. If you have a subsidized Stafford loan, you will not be charged interest during the deferment period. However, if your loan is unsubsidized, you will be responsible for paying the interest that is due on the loan during that period. If you cannot afford to pay it, the interest will accumulate and will be added to your outstanding loan balance.

You may be entitled to a loan deferment if you are:

● Unemployed.

● Experiencing an economic hardship.

● Teaching in an area where there is a shortage of teachers.

● Disabled.

● On active duty in the military.

● On parental leave from your job or are the mother of preschool students.

If you are experiencing a temporary problem repaying your education loan and you are not eligible for a deferment, you may be eligible for forbearance. During forbearance, you will either make no payments at all on your loan or you will make smaller payments. However, you will have to pay interest during the forbearance period regardless of whether your Stafford loan is subsidized or unsubsidized. If you can't afford to pay the interest it will accumulate during the forbearance period and will be added to your loan balance.

You may be eligible for a discharge of your student loan if you:

- Are unable to pay due to poor health or some other unforeseen event.

- Become disabled or die.

- Serve in the military.

- Are employed full-time as a nurse, medical technician, law enforcement officer or corrections officer.

- Are a teacher in a low-income area and teach handicapped children or teach specific subjects.

- Decide to return to school on at least a half-time basis.

- Were defrauded by a career or vocational school.

For specific information on your eligibility for a deferment or forbearance, contact the Direct Loan Servicing Center if you have a Direct Stafford loan. The phone number for the Center is 1-800-848-0979 or 315-738-6634. You can also contact the center at *www.dlservicer.ed.gov*. If you have a FFEL Stafford loan contact the lender or agency that holds your loan to discuss a deferment.

For information about your options when you can't afford to repay your Perkins student loan, contact the agency or private lender that made the loan.

For specific information on all of your options when you can't keep up with your student loan obligations, call your student loan lender or loan servicer, or go to *www.sfahelp.ed.gov* at the Department of Education's Web site, or call the DOE's Federal Student Aid Information Center at 1-800-433-3243.

If you default on your student loan, the full amount of the loan will be due immediately. If you do not pay it, the DOE may ask the IRS to intercept any individual income tax refunds you are entitled to and apply that money to the loan balance, or your employer may be ordered to begin deducting money from your paychecks to pay off the debt.

You will be liable for all of the DOE's collection expenses related to your student loan, and if you decide to return to school in the future, you will not be entitled to receive any more federal student aid. For more information on what to do when you default on your government student loan, read the DOE's *Guide to Defaulted Student Loans,* which is available at www.ed.gov. You can also order the guide by calling 1-800-433-3243.

Your Child-Support Obligation

Federal and state governments have become increasingly serious about cracking down on parents who don't pay their court-ordered child support and in recent years have acquired more and more powerful collection tools. Once you fall behind on your child-support obligation, the child-support enforcement office in your state, which is a part of your state attorney general's office, will contact you to try to collect what you owe. If you don't pay up, it may:

- Garnish your wages.

- Seize your property.

- Take away your professional license.

- Put liens on your property.

- Collect the money you owe from other sources of income you may receive, such as Supplemental Security Income (SSI), Workmen's Compensation, unemployment, insurance proceeds, and any money you may win in a lawsuit.

- Declare you in contempt of court and put you in jail.

Also, the parent who is entitled to the support may hire an attorney or a child-support collection agency to collect the money from you.

Schedule a meeting with the lawyer who helped you negotiate the terms of your divorce or with another family law attorney as soon as you know that you can't afford to continue making your child-support payments. The attorney will help you file a "Request for Modification" with the court. Then, a judge will decide whether or not you have a legitimate reason for making smaller child-support payments. If the judge decides that you do, she may lower the size of your payments permanently or temporarily depending on the circumstances.

Your Federal Income Taxes

The IRS has almost unlimited collection powers. For example, it can take your home in payment for your tax debt, even if your state's property exemptions protect your home from other collection actions. Therefore, if you cannot pay your taxes, don't sit back and hope that the IRS won't notice that you have fallen behind. Sooner or later it will. Instead, file your tax return by April 15 and at the same time, let the IRS know that you would like to do one of the following:

- Work out a plan for paying your tax debt in installments. If you do not owe the IRS more than $10,000 and if you are current on all your previous tax obligations, the IRS will give you an automatic installment plan—no questions asked—if you ask for one. To request the plan, file IRS Form 9465 with your tax return. You will be charged a $43 fee for the plan, the cost of which will be added to your tax balance.

  If you owe more than $10,000, you must get special permission from the IRS to pay your taxes in installments. After you request an installment plan, the IRS will review your financial information to confirm that you really need one and to determine how much you can afford to pay each month. To get the best deal, hire a CPA or another tax professional to help you. They understand how the IRS works and can help you negotiate with the agency.

  You are not eligible for an installment plan if you already had one during the previous five years and if you failed to file one or more of your tax returns and/or to pay any taxes that were due during that time period.

  While your installment plan is in effect, you must make

all of your payments on time. If you fall behind, the IRS will give you a couple of chances to catch up, and, if you don't, it will begin the collection process. You must also pay interest and penalties on your outstanding tax debt while the plan is in effect. Those payments will substantially increase the total amount of money you end up paying to the IRS over the length of your installment plan. Therefore, before you ask for an installment plan, make certain that there is not a less expensive way to pay the taxes that you owe. You can find out the terms of the installment agreement you will qualify for by entering the Interactive Installment Payment Process section of the IRS Web site at *www.irs.gov*. If you do not meet all of your future tax obligations while your installment plan is in effect, the plan will be canceled.

> ## Watch Out!
>
> If you need more time to prepare your tax return, file an "Application for Automatic Extension of Time to File" no later than April 15. You will automatically get an extension to file until August 15. However, the extension does *not* apply to the income taxes you may owe—you must pay the full amount of the taxes you *think* you owe by April 15. Once you are ready to file your return and have figured out exactly how much tax you actually owe, you may have to pay the IRS more in taxes or you may get a tax refund.

● Negotiate an "Offer in Compromise" (OIC). An OIC involves paying the IRS less than the full amount of the taxes that you owe in order to get rid of your tax debt. You will also have to pay interest and penalties on your outstanding tax debt.

To make an offer, complete IRS Form 6656 and indicate on the form exactly how much money you want to pay to settle your tax debt. You must also file IRS Form 433-A to provide the IRS with detailed information about your finances.

To get an OIC from the IRS, you must convince the agency that there is no way that you can afford to pay everything that you owe, now or in the future, and that if the IRS tries to collect your tax debt, you will suffer an "undue hardship." Therefore, don't try to handle your own OIC request. You need professional assistance from start to finish.

If you reach an agreement with the IRS, you must either pay the full amount of your OIC within 90 days, or the IRS will let you pay that amount off over several years. However, the longer you take to pay it, the more the debt will cost you, since you will be paying interest and penalties during the payment period. Also, if you do not live up to your OIC agreement, the IRS can hold you liable for all of your unpaid taxes and can take immediate action to collect what you owe.

> **Watch Out!**
>
> As part of the OIC process, you must file any tax returns from the past that you did not file. If you owe taxes on any of those returns, the IRS will take those debts into account when it decides what is a fair amount for you to pay.

If the IRS rejects your offer, you can make another one, you can appeal the agency's decision within 30 days of receiving its rejection notice, or you can file for bankruptcy. Filing for bankruptcy buys you time to figure out what to do about your tax debt. You can also do nothing, but the IRS will use all of its collection powers to get the money it is entitled to.

When a Debt Collector Calls

While you are trying to figure out what to do about your debts, debt collectors may begin calling you to find out when you are going to pay the money that you owe. Since their income depends on how much they collect from you, debt collectors can be very persistent. Some may even use scare tactics and verbal abuse to get you to pay up.

Don't be cowed into paying a debt just because a debt collector puts pressure on you. The debt he is trying to collect may be low priority. Chapter 2 distinguished between high priority and low priority debts. Also, depending on how the debt collector applies the pressure, he may be violating your legal rights under the federal Fair Debt Collection Practices Act (FDCPA). For example, the law says that a debt collector cannot:

● Try to deceive you or scare you into paying a debt by sending you a letter that looks like it came from a government agency or court or by implying that he is a government agent.

● Threaten to harm you, your reputation, or your property or threaten to put you in jail. However, a debt collector can threaten to garnish your wages or seize your property, assuming that garnishments and seizures are legal in your state and that the collector fully intends to act on his threat.

● Call you repeatedly or use insulting, abusive, or obscene language when he speaks to you.

● Contact you at work if you let him know that your employer does not want you to be contacted there.

● Contact your employer about the money you owe unless the debt collector is trying to collect your past-due child-support payments.

● Contact your friends, family members, or neighbors about the money you owe without your permission or the court's authorization.

The FDCPA also says that:

Money$ense

The FDCPA applies to debt-collection firms and to attorneys who collect debts, but not to creditors' own in-house debt collectors. However, most states have their own debt-collections laws and some state laws apply to in-house debt collectors. Contact your state attorney general's office to find out about the law in your state.

● A debt collector can contact you by mail, by phone, telegram, or in person about the money that you owe. However, he cannot contact you about your debt using a postcard or any other form of mail that might let people know that the correspondence is from a debt collector.

● A debt collector can only call you between 8 a.m. and 9 p.m., unless you indicate that there is a better time to get in touch. He cannot call you anytime on a Sunday.

● Within five days of contacting you for the first time about the debt that a debt collector says you owe, the collector must mail you a formal written notice about the debt. The notice must indicate exactly how much you owe, to whom you owe it, your right to request written verification of the debt, and your right to dispute the debt.

How to Respond to a Debt Collector

When a debt collector contacts you about a debt, you can respond in one of several ways:

- Arrange to pay the debt in a lump sum or in installments, assuming you agree that you owe the debt and that you can pay it without jeopardizing your ability to pay your top-priority debts. If you want to pay the debt over time, do not let the debt collector pressure you into paying more than you can afford.

- Ask the debt collector for written verification of the debt when you know that you owe the money but want time to figure out what to do about it. You should also ask for written debt verification when you are not sure that you owe the money, or question the amount of the debt.

- Write the debt collector a letter stating that you do not want to be contacted about the debt again. According to the FDCPA, after receiving your letter the debt collector cannot contact you other than to confirm that your letter was received or to tell you about a collection action he is about to take. However, if the debt that the debt collector is trying to collect is relatively small, the creditor he is working for may decide to write it off as uncollectible after you send your letter.

- Write the debt collector a letter stating that you do not owe the money he is trying to

Watch Out!

If one of your creditors writes off your debt as uncollectible, that damaging information may end up in your credit record.

collect from you and that you don't want to be contacted about it again. Make sure that your letter is postmarked no more than 30 days after you were first contacted about the debt. Send the letter certified mail and ask for a return receipt. By law, once the debt collector receives your letter, he cannot contact you again other than to send you information that proves you owe the money. Meanwhile, however, collection actions can still move forward, but you won't be contacted about them.

Be careful how much information you share with a debt collector. The information could be used against you later. Do not lie, but do not offer any information that you are not asked about and never share information about your bank account or about your other assets. If a debt collector asks you about them, politely let him know that you will not answer his questions.

If a debt collector violates your federal or state debt-collection rights or if the debt he is trying to collect is substantial and/or is collateralized by your home or some other important asset, hire a consumer law attorney. You should also hire an attorney if you are sued by a debt collector. Let the debt collector know as soon as you hire the attorney. At that point, the debt collector must stop contacting you and deal with your attorney instead. You should also contact an attorney if a debt collector threatens you with a lawsuit.

Under the FDCPA you can sue a debt collector for actual as well as punitive damages. Actual dam-

Money$ense

When a debt collector violates your legal rights, file a complaint with the Federal Trade Commission (FTC), the agency that enforces the FDCPA, and with your state attorney general's office of consumer protection too, if your state has its own debt-collection law.

ages represent compensation for the harm you suffered. For example, you may be compensated for out-of-pocket costs, lost wages, et cetera, as well as for the pain and suffering you may have experienced because of the debt collector's actions. Punitive damages are awarded to discourage a lawbreaker from breaking the law again. If you win your lawsuit, you may also receive up to $1,000 as compensation for the debt collector's misconduct, and the debt collector will have to pay your attorney's fees and expenses. If you have a strong case against a debt collector, an attorney is likely to represent you on a contingent-fee basis.

6

HOW TO KEEP YOUR WHEELS ON THE ROAD AND THE ROOF OVER YOUR HEAD

Falling behind on your car payments, monthly rent obligation, or mortgage loan is no laughing matter. You could lose your transportation to and from work as well as the roof over your head. Your credit record will be seriously damaged as well. Therefore, this chapter provides strategies for how to avoid a repossession, foreclosure, or eviction when there is a threat of one. It also lays out your options for what to do once one has begun. The chapter also explains how a consumer law attorney can help you.

Strategies to Avoid a Repossession

One morning, you head out the door, ready to drive off to work. But when you look toward the driveway, you notice that your car is nowhere in sight. Where did it go? If you have missed just a few payments on your car loan—maybe even one, depending on your state—your car may have been repossessed. In most states, missing three payments in a row is all it takes to trigger repossession. The lender can take your car without notifying you ahead of time about what is going to happen, without giving you a chance to get caught up on your loan so you can keep your car, and without suing you first to get the court's permission to take your car.

Watch Out!

When you are behind on your car payments, your loan agreement may give the lender the right to call your loan—demand that you pay the loan in full immediately or lose your car—even after you pay the past-due amount. If your loan agreement includes this provision, before you pay the past-due loan balance, ask the lender to agree in writing to waive that right.

Obviously the best way to avoid repossession is to make your car payments on time and to get in touch with your lender as soon as you realize that you are going to have trouble making them. If you have a history of timely payments and you are sure that your financial problems will be short-lived, the lender may agree to let you make interest-only payments or smaller loan payments for a while. However, if your finances have suffered a serious setback, you may request that the lender permanently reduce the size of your loan payments. Chapter 5 offers strategies and advice for negotiating with creditors.

If your lender is willing to negotiate a new debt-payment

agreement with you, don't sign it until you understand all of the terms of the agreement. For example, if the lender agrees to let you make reduced payments for the next six months, be sure that you are clear about how you will make up the difference between what you would have paid on the loan during those months and what you will actually pay. The agreement may require you to pay the difference in a lump sum at the end of the six months or at the end of the term of your loan, or it may indicate that the amount will be added to your total loan balance. You should also be clear about whether or not you will have to make a balloon payment at the end of the new debt-payment agreement. If you can't make the payment when it comes due, you will once again be in jeopardy of losing your car, but at that point you will have invested even more of your money in it.

Sell Your Car

Rather than negotiating with your creditor to keep your car, you may be better off selling it and using the proceeds to pay off your loan. Selling it can be a good option if:

- The car is not your main mode of transportation.

- You do not have a lot of money invested in your car.

- The car is too expensive for you to own and operate when you take into account how much you are spending to insure it, keep it gassed up, and to get it serviced and repaired in addition to the size of your monthly loan payments.

If repossession is in the offing, selling your car offers a couple of advantages. First, you avoid having repossession on your credit record. Second, you will likely get more for your car than if the lender repossesses and sells your car in a public auction and proceeds of the auction are applied to your loan balance. If the proceeds are not enough to pay the balance in full, you will have to pay the deficiency.

Give Your Car Back

When you give your car back to the lender, it is called a voluntary repossession. Once you do, the lender will sell the car and use the sale proceeds to pay off your loan balance. If you are concerned that the car may not sell for enough to wipe out the full outstanding balance on your car loan, before you give it back, ask the lender to forgive any potential deficiency in exchange for the return of your car. Since you are saving the lender from having to incur the costs of taking back your car, it may agree to your request. You should also ask the lender not to report the voluntary repossession to the credit bureaus it works with. If the lender agrees to make any concessions, be sure to get them in writing before you return your car.

File for Bankruptcy

You can use bankruptcy to stop repossession and to give yourself time to figure out what to do about your car loan. You may even be able to use bankruptcy to get your car back after it has been repossessed, but before it has been sold.

A Chapter 7 liquidation bankruptcy gets rid of all of your unsecured debt and gives you an opportunity to hold on to your car by continuing to make your car payments. A Chapter 13 reorganization bankruptcy gives you three to five years to pay off the balance on your car loan through monthly installments. Chapter 7 explains how each type of bankruptcy works.

How a Consumer Law Attorney Can Help

If your efforts to negotiate more affordable debt-payment plans with your car (or home) lender are unsuccessful, you don't want to give up your car (or house), and you are worried that a repossession (or foreclosure) may be imminent, schedule an appointment with a consumer law attorney. He can figure out if the lender has violated any laws related to your loan or to the loan-collection process or has made any mistakes related to your loan. The attorney may be able to use that information to halt or delay the repossession (or foreclosure) and in some situations, he can even stop the process after it has begun. For example, the lender may have:

- Made errors in your loan paperwork

- Not properly perfected its lien on your loan collateral

- Breached your loan agreement in some way

- Violated state or federal debt-collection laws

The attorney may also recommend that you sue your lender, which could mean money in your pocket if you win the lawsuit.

The attorney will represent you on a contingent-fee basis if he believes that you have a good chance of winning the lawsuit.

A consumer law attorney can also advise you about what to do and not do when the "repo man" comes for your car, including how to stop the repossession without violating the law.

To find a qualified consumer law attorney, ask the National Consumer Law Center (NCLC) in Boston for a referral. The center's phone number is 617-523-8089. Another source of referrals is the National Association of Consumer Advocates, in Washington, D.C., at 1-202-452-1989. Some bankruptcy attorneys are consumer attorneys.

Money$ense

If you are worried that your vehicle may be repossessed, remove from it all of your personal items, including any extras you may have installed in your vehicle after you bought it, such as a CD player, television, VCR, and so on. Although you are legally entitled to get back any personal items that may be in your car when it is repossessed, the truth is, you may never get them. If your car is repossessed with some of your personal belongings in it, send the lender a letter right away demanding that they be returned immediately. In the letter list each of the items that you want back.

When Repossession Happens

Sometimes, no matter how hard you try to avoid it, it happens—repossession. When your car is about to be repossessed, a repo man will come to your home, your place of business, or to somewhere else to take it away. If the repo man comes to your home, he is entitled to step onto your property to take your car, but he cannot break into your locked garage to get your car. Beware, in some states it is illegal to hide your car to avoid repossession.

In most states the repo man cannot "breach the peace" in

order to take your car. In other words, he cannot threaten you with bodily harm or physical violence, among other things. A consumer law attorney may be able to get your car back for you if the repo man breaches the peace.

If you are present when your car is about to be repossessed and if you verbally object to having it taken by loudly saying something like, "Do not take my car!" the repo man is legally prohibited from taking it at that time. However, he could repossess your car some other time when you are not around.

Your car will be sold at a public auction after it is repossessed. You will be notified about the date, time, and location of the auction so you can try to buy your car if you want. If you do not buy it back, the sale proceeds will be applied to the outstanding balance on your loan. If you are lucky, the proceeds will be sufficient to pay off the loan's outstanding balance *and* to reimburse the lender for the costs of taking your car, storing it, and selling it. Otherwise, you will owe the difference. However, if the deficiency is small, the lender may be willing to forgive the deficiency or let you pay it off over time.

Depending on the law in your state, you may be entitled to reinstate your loan and get your car back before it is sold. To do that however, you will either have to pay the past-due balance or the entire loan balance in a lump sum as well as the full amount of the lender's repossession costs.

How to Hold On to Your Home When You Are Worried About a Foreclosure

Losing your home because you can't keep up with your mortgage payments is every home owner's worst nightmare. Not only will you have to give up what is probably your most valuable asset, but you will also forfeit all of the equity you have in it. Furthermore, even if your financial situation turns around, during the seven years that the foreclosure is in your credit record it will be tough to qualify for a new mortgage loan at reasonable terms so that you can purchase another home.

Luckily mortgage lenders don't like to take back homes, because of the expense of the foreclosure process and because they end up with a house that they have to spend more money on to get rid of. Therefore, if you contact your lender sooner rather than later—preferably before you have begun to fall behind on your mortgage payments—the lender may bend over backward to help you keep your home, assuming that your finances are not in really bad shape.

Don't overlook the option of scheduling an appointment with a consumer law attorney when you are worried about a foreclosure. Also, be open to the possibility that giving up your home may be your best option, despite how much you have invested in it financially and emotionally.

Money$ense

If your loan is serviced by a loan-servicing company, not by your mortgage lender, you may have to renegotiate the terms of your mortgage loan with the loan servicer. However, your lender will probably have the final say on the terms of any new agreement you may reach.

What to Do When a Foreclosure Begins

When you are one month behind on your mortgage loan, you will probably receive a polite notice from your lender reminding you that the payment is past due and indicating how much you must pay in late fees. If you miss three consecutive mortgage payments, however, the lender may report your delinquency to the credit bureaus it works with and will probably send you a "Notice of Default"—your official notification that a foreclosure has begun. Among other things, the Notice of Default will indicate the number of loan payments that you have missed and the total amount that is past due.

Schedule an appointment with a consumer law attorney immediately! The attorney can help you figure out what to do next. Depending on your situation, he may refer you to a bankruptcy attorney. Don't try to deal with your mortgage delinquency yourself. Your mortgage lender knows a whole lot more about your loan and about the foreclosure process than you do, so you will be at a disadvantage if you try to go it alone. A skilled, knowledgeable attorney can help level the playing field and increase the likelihood that you will be able to hold on to your home, if you decide that is your best option.

After you have received the Notice of Default, you will probably have a couple of months to either pay the amount that you owe or to negotiate a new debt-payment plan so that you can keep your home. However, the specific amount of time that you have will depend on whether foreclosures in your state are *judicial* or *statutory*. Your state attorney general's office of consumer affairs can tell you which kind of foreclosure applies to your state.

If foreclosures in your state are judicial, your mortgage lender must sue you to get the court's permission to take back your home. Since lawsuits take time to resolve, you will have considerable time to either come up with the money you need to keep your home or to work out some other way to avoid a foreclosure after the lawsuit begins.

On the other hand, if your state law provides for statutory foreclosures, there will be no lawsuit and no court involvement—it is an administrative process only. Most likely, all your mortgage holder has to do to take back your home is advertise that it is for sale in your local newspaper, send you some written notices, and give you a certain amount of time to pay what you owe. Therefore, in a statutory foreclosure, you could lose your home very quickly if you don't have the money to slow down or stop the process.

If you disagree with the amount that the Notice of Default says you owe, the attorney you are working with may suggest trying to stop the foreclosure dead in its tracks by giving your mortgage lender a check for the amount that you think you owe. The attorney will prepare a letter to be sent with the check. The letter will state that the check represents the amount of money you believe you owe in past-due mortgage payments and that by accepting your check, the mortgage lender is agreeing that you have paid your mortgage arrearage in full, and, therefore, it will stop the foreclosure process. If the difference between the amount of your check and the amount of the arrearage indicated on the Notice of Default is not substantial, your lender may agree to the terms of your letter.

Another option for stopping a foreclosure and holding on to your home is to restructure the loan so you can afford to pay it.

Watch Out!

If you wait too long to contact your mortgage lender after you have fallen behind on your mortgage payments, regulations and loan servicing guidelines may limit your options for holding on to your home.

Your attorney will handle the negotiations for you. As a part of the negotiations, the attorney may ask your mortgage holder to:

● Lower your mortgage payments for a limited period of time. Your lender will want to know when you can resume making the regular payments and how you will pay off your past-due mortgage balance. One option is to add the balance to the end of your loan so that you won't have to worry about paying the past-due amount right away. However, there may be a limit on the number of missed payments you can add to the end of the loan. Another option is to pay the past-due balance over time.

● Permanently restructure the terms of your loan. Among other things, your attorney may ask your lender to do all or some of the following:

- Lower the interest rate
- Extend the length of the loan
- Cancel some of the loan principal
- Capitalize the amount that is past due so you pay it off over time

● Refinance your mortgage. Refinancing may make sense if there has been a significant drop in mortgage interest rates since you got your mortgage.

Another option, if your loan is insured by the Federal Housing Administration (FHA), is to apply to have your mortgage loan transferred to the federal Housing and Urban Development Department (HUD). HUD will help you work out a plan for getting caught up on your mortgage. However, to qualify for a transfer you have to prove that an illness, a sudden job loss, or some other problem beyond your control has caused you to fall behind on your mortgage, and you must be able to resume making your regular mortgage payments within 36 months. You can obtain a mortgage transfer application from your lender or from the HUD office in your area. You can find the phone number in the government listings section of your local phone book.

If you do nothing after you receive a Notice of Default, regardless of whether foreclosures in your state are judicial or statutory, the foreclosure process will move forward and the next notice you receive will be a "Notice of Acceleration." This notice demands that you pay the full outstanding balance on your mortgage, not just the amount that is past due, by a specified date. If you are not already working with an attorney, hire one immediately!

Deed Back Your Home or Sell It

If your lender won't negotiate with you or if your negotiations fail, you can still avoid having a foreclosure on your credit record by selling your home or by deeding it back to the lender. Selling your home and using the proceeds to pay off your mortgage can be a good option if you have a lot of equity in your home and the real estate market is strong.

Before you agree to sell your home, make sure that your lender will put the foreclosure on hold while your home is on the market. Also, find out if the lender will accept the sale proceeds as payment in full should your home sell for less than what you owe on it. You will be responsible for paying the deficiency otherwise. Get in writing all of the terms and conditions of your agreement with the lender.

Deeding your home back to your mortgage lender makes sense when you do not have much equity in your home, and especially if the real estate market in your area is soft. In a soft market, it could take a very long time to sell your home or your home could sell for a lot less than what you owe on it.

> **Money$ense**
>
> If your mortgage is assumable, you may be able to avoid a foreclosure by finding someone to take over the loan. However, even if it is not assumable, your lender may agree to an assumption to avoid the cost of taking back your home and so it can begin receiving income from the loan again.

If You Lose Your Home

> **Money$ense**
>
> Never agree to deed back your home without trying to get a concession or two from your mortgage lender first. Your lawyer will know what concessions to ask for.

If the foreclosure moves forward and your mortgage lender takes back title to your home, you will receive a "Notice of Sale" telling you when your home will go on the auction block. The sale proceeds will be applied to the balance on your mortgage and to the lender's foreclosure costs. If there is money left over, it will go to satisfy any liens that other creditors may have on your home, and then to you.

If your home sells for less than what you owe on it, the lender will demand that you pay the difference by a certain date. If you can't come up with the money, the lender may try to collect it. However, the lender may decide to forgive the debt if it is not enough to sue you for.

Beware! If there seems to be no way for you to hold on to your home, your emotions may take over and you may be vulnerable to the promises of shady businesses who prey on people in your situation. Although they may tell you that they want to help, they are really out to get your home. Therefore, before you agree to work with an unfamiliar business that tells you it can help you hold on to your home, check it out with the consumer protection office of your attorney general and with the Federal Trade Commission (FTC). Only work with lenders who are 100 percent reputable.

What to Do When You Are Behind on Your Rent

When you fall behind on your rent, you are defaulting on or breaking your lease agreement. Therefore, your landlord has a legal right to evict you after giving you a chance to move out voluntarily. Your lease states how many rent payments you must miss to be in default.

Talk with your landlord as soon as you know you are going to have problems making your rent payments. If you know that your financial problems are temporary, the landlord may agree to let you make smaller rent payments for a period of time. Make sure you discuss how you will make up the difference between what you pay and what you would have paid.

If you have no idea when your financial situation will improve, you can avoid an eviction by breaking your lease and moving into some place less expensive.

Money$ense

If you need help figuring out how to respond to a possible eviction notice, contact your local tenant's organization for free assistance or meet with a landlord-tenant attorney.

Read your lease before you do, however, so that you understand the potential financial and legal consequences of taking that step.

Depending on the terms of the lease, you may have to pay a penalty for breaking it and you may have to give your landlord 30-days' notice. In addition, the lease probably obligates you to continue making your rent payments after you move out until your landlord finds a tenant to replace you. Under certain conditions, your landlord may even have the right to sue you for breaking your lease. If your lease is almost up and you will lose your deposit if you break your lease, you may be better off finishing out the lease and not renewing.

If you decide to break your lease, speak to your landlord about your plans and find out if she will waive any penalties you may be obligated to pay as well as her right to sue you, assuming your lease gives your landlord that right. If your local rental market is strong and if your landlord feels confident that she can find a new tenant quickly, she may agree to your requests. If your landlord makes any concessions, get them in writing.

Money$ense

Finding a tenant to replace you before you tell your landlord that you want to break your lease may increase the likelihood that your landlord will agree to any of the concessions you ask for.

Subletting is another option when you can't afford to pay your rent, assuming your lease allows it. When you sublet the place that you are renting, you rent it to someone else. However, if the person who subleases from you falls behind on the rent or damages the rental unit, your landlord is legally entitled to look to you for the missed rent payments and to pay for the cost of the repairs. Therefore, don't agree to sublease to anyone unless you are sure that the individual can afford the rent and is a responsible tenant. Always use a sublease agreement to spell out the terms and conditions of the sublease.

Your lease may allow you to assign it to someone else. In that case, unlike a sublease arrangement, once you sign your lease over to the new tenant, all of your lease-related legal obligations end.

How an Eviction Begins

Prior to the start of an eviction, you will receive a written notice from your landlord informing you that you are in default of your lease. The notice will tell you how much you must pay to get caught up on your rent and how many days you have to come up with the money. It will also tell you that if you do not pay the money by the deadline, you must move out within a certain number of days.

If you disagree with the amount of past-due rent that your landlord says you owe, write your landlord a polite letter stating how much you think you really owe. In the letter, refer to any documentation you may have that helps prove your point—canceled rent checks for example—and attach copies of the documentation to your letter. Mail the letter certified mail, return receipt requested. If your landlord decides that you are correct, get it in writing.

If you cannot work out a way to continue living in your rental unit, start looking for a more affordable place to live and let your landlord know in writing what you are doing. If you decide that you can't be out by the vacate date on the notice, ask if you can stay a little longer. If your landlord agrees, get it in writing.

When you move out, you will be responsible for paying your landlord all of the past-due rent that you owe. If you paid a security deposit, the landlord will deduct what you owe from your deposit. However, if the deposit is not sufficient to cover the full amount of the past-due rent, you will be responsible for paying the difference. Your landlord may let you pay the amount over time, in installments. If you don't pay it, your landlord may sue you for the money.

After your landlord deducts from your deposit the full amount of your past-due rent and any other expenses she is legally entitled to be reimbursed for, you are entitled to receive any money that may be left over.

After You Receive a Summons

If your eviction moves forward, you will be served with a legal notice called a summons. It is your official notice that you have been sued for eviction. The summons may also indicate the date of your eviction trial, which will occur in your area's small claims court, in a special housing court, or in some other low-level, relatively informal court.

Get legal help as soon as you are served with the summons. Don't try to handle things yourself. Possible sources of legal help include your local tenant's organization, a landlord-tenant attorney who is willing to represent you for free or for a reduced fee, and your area's Legal Aid office. Legal Aid is a federally funded program that offers legal assistance to low-income people. If you do not find a listing for Legal Aid in your local phone book, call the Legal Services Corporation in Washington, D.C., at 202-336-8800.

There are several ways to respond to your landlord's lawsuit. You can:

Watch Out!

If your eviction will be heard in small claims court, you may not be able to have an attorney represent you in the courtroom. You will have to act as your own attorney. Call the court clerk to find out.

● Fight the eviction by filing a written answer or response by the indicated deadline. In your answer, you can disagree with what the landlord alleges in the lawsuit. You may also have the basis for a countersuit against your landlord.

● Settle with your landlord out of court in exchange for having the lawsuit dropped.

● Show up in court on the day of the trial. Check with the court clerk to make sure that you can show up without filing any paperwork first.

● Not respond to the summons and not show up in court. The court will probably award your landlord a default judgment, which means that the landlord will automatically get permission to kick you out of your rental unit. Your landlord will deduct from your security deposit all of his court costs and the full amount of past-due rent that you owe. He may sue you if the deposit is not enough to pay everything.

Money$ense

Your landlord is breaking the law if he tries to make you move by changing your locks, threatening you, or getting your utilities cut off. Get in touch with your local tenant's organization, or with a landlord-tenant attorney if your landlord does any of these things.

If your landlord wins the right to evict you, you can appeal the court's decision and put the eviction on hold. If you don't appeal, and if you do not pay your landlord what you owe, a county peace officer—a constable, sheriff, or marshal depending on where you live—will notify you in person about when the eviction will take place. The peace officer will return to your home on that date to move out your belongings if you are not already moved out.

7

BANKRUPTCY: YOUR OPTION OF LAST RESORT

Gail Lewis was beside herself. Two years ago, she divorced her husband, Gabriel, and she got their home as part of the settlement agreement. Gail had primary custody of their two kids and felt that it would help them adjust to the divorce if they could continue living in the only home they had known. However, she had not realized what a struggle it would be to come up with the mortgage payment every month, much less pay for the home's upkeep and maintenance as well as for its insurance and property taxes. On top of that, her ex-husband did not always pay his child support on time, so sometimes Gail had to use credit cards to help her pay her living expenses. Now, she was behind on many of her debts and had begun to receive threatening notices from her mortgage lender. At first she had tried to ignore the notices because she did not know what to do and felt so overwhelmed by her financial situation, but then she received a notice about her home loan that really scared her. It sounded like the mortgage lender was going to take her house from her. That night Gail dreamed that she and her two children were living in their car because the mortgage company had kicked them out of their home.

The next morning Gail decided to call the attorney who had helped her with her divorce to ask what she should do. The divorce attorney gave Gail the name of a bankruptcy attorney and told Gail to call the attorney right away. Gail followed her advice.

Three days later, Gail met with the attorney to discuss her financial situation and to review her options for dealing with her mortgage loan. The attorney advised Gail to file Chapter 13 bankruptcy and explained how it would help her. He also told Gail that he thought she should be open to selling her home and moving into some place that was less expensive.

After thinking about the attorney's advice for a week and talking it over with her best friend, Gail decided that bankruptcy was her best option, even though she hated the idea of having to file. She also came to terms with the idea of selling her house. She knew that it would sell for a lot of money, since it was attractive and located in a very desirable neighborhood, and she was confident that she could find a nice place to rent in the same neighborhood that would cost her less each month. Not having to worry about repairs and maintenance and property taxes would be a big relief.

Bankruptcy—just the thought of it may make you break out in a cold sweat. Filing for bankruptcy—that's something that other people do—not you! However, filing for bankruptcy can be a smart move when you are drowning in debt and have not been able to work things out with your creditors or figure out a financially sensible way to consolidate your debt. Bankruptcy may be your best move if you are being threatened with a fore-closure or repossession, with the loss of your utility service, the garnishment of your wages, or with some other creditor collec-tion action. Consult with a bankruptcy attorney to see if it's the right move for you.

Bankruptcy is a legal process governed by federal law. It stops most, but not all, creditor collection actions and gives you time to figure out how to deal with your debts. Bankruptcy helps you get rid of some, but not all of your unsecured debts and, de-pending on the type of bankruptcy that you file, may help you lower some of your monthly debt payments. However, you may also have to give up some of your assets. They will be sold and the proceeds will be used to pay off your debts.

Most consumers file one of two different types of bankruptcy: a *reorganization* or Chapter 13 bankruptcy, or a *liquidation* or Chapter 7 bankruptcy. This chapter explains how each type of bankruptcy works and reviews the various decisions you must make as you work your way through the bankruptcy process.

Beginning a Bankruptcy

Hire an experienced bankruptcy attorney to help you with your bankruptcy. The process is too complicated to handle on your own. If you file Chapter 13, an attorney will charge between $750 and $3,000. If you file Chapter 7, the assistance of an at-torney will run between $500 and $2,500. The exact amount that you have to pay will depend on the complexity of your bank-ruptcy and on what area of the country you live in.

Among other things, the bankruptcy attorney will:

● Help you determine the type of bankruptcy you should file.

● Complete all of your bankruptcy paperwork.

● File your bankruptcy petition and pay the filing fee.

● Deal with your creditors as necessary—some of them may be upset that you have filed for bankruptcy.

● Represent you at the creditors' meetings and other court hearings.

● Help you make decisions throughout the bankruptcy process.

You begin your bankruptcy by filing a petition and some other legal forms with the federal bankruptcy court in your area. The other forms include a "statement of affairs" and schedules of your assets and debts. If you are filing a Chapter 13 bankruptcy, you must also file a debt reorganization plan, which explains how you intend to deal with each of your debts.

Money$ense

In some states, bankruptcy attorneys are board certified. This means that they have passed a special state bankruptcy exam in addition to passing their state's bar exam and that they stay up-to-date on the latest changes in bankruptcy law by taking periodic classes.

You must pay the court a filing fee when you file a bankruptcy petition. Although the amount of the fee changes periodically, at the time this book was written the fee for a Chapter 13 was $185 and $200 for a Chapter 7.

The filing of your bankruptcy petition will establish an "automatic stay." This means that the court and your attorney will send your creditors proof that you have filed and your creditors will be legally obligated to suspend all of their efforts to collect from you.

Bankruptcy Don'ts

During the months immediately prior to filing for Chapter 13 or 7, doing certain things will complicate your bankruptcy and make it difficult for you to get the maximum benefit out of filing. For example, you may have to pay more of your debts than you would have to pay otherwise after your bankruptcy is over and you could even end up in legal trouble. Therefore, do not:

● Conceal assets from the bankruptcy court by transferring their ownership to someone else. If the trustee discovers what you have done, he will include those assets in your bankruptcy and you may lose them as a result. Also, you may be charged with fraud.

● Get a cash advance of more than $1,150 within 60 days of filing for bankruptcy.

● Charge more than $1,150 in luxury goods or services—anything that is not essential to your life—with one creditor within 60 days of filing. If one of your creditors objects to the charges and the bankruptcy judge upholds the objection, the debt will be yours to pay when your bankruptcy is over.

● Pay one creditor at the expense of another within 90 days of filing for bankruptcy. The trustee can void your payment and distribute the money more fairly among your creditors.

● Give a creditor a postdated check. If the check bounces, you could be criminally prosecuted. Your bankruptcy will not protect you from having to pay any legal fines you may be assessed.

Chapter 13 Bankruptcy

Chapter 13 bankruptcy helps you hold on to your assets by reducing your monthly debt payments and giving you between three and five years to pay what you owe. During those years, you will be protected from your creditors as long as you meet all of the terms of your debt reorganization plan. Specifically, you can use Chapter 13 to:

● Keep your exempt and nonexempt assets. Exempt assets are assets that are legally protected from the collection actions of your creditors. Nonexempt assets are not protected, but you may be able to keep them by paying the creditors with liens on those assets the value of their liens. The federal bankruptcy law provides a list of assets you can exempt and also sets a dollar limit on the total value of the assets you can exempt. Individual states have their own lists of exemptions and dollar limits, and 13 states let you choose between the federal exemptions and their own exemptions. The exemption laws in Florida and Texas are extremely generous.

● Reduce the total amount of money that you have to pay to some of your secured creditors.

● Get rid of some, but not all of your debts.

You are a good candidate for a Chapter 13 bankruptcy if you have a stable job and a steady income. However, you cannot use this type of bankruptcy to reorganize if you owe more than $290,525 in unsecured debt or more than $871,550 in secured debt. (These dollar limits change periodically due to cost-of-living increases.) Instead, if you want to reorganize your debts you will have to file a Chapter 11 reorganization bankruptcy, which is more expensive than a Chapter 13 and more difficult to complete.

> **Money$ense**
>
> Filing a Chapter 13 bankruptcy does less damage to your credit record than filing for Chapter 7 because you pay more of what you owe. In fact, although federal law says that both types of bankruptcies can remain in your credit record for ten years, the three national credit bureaus, Equifax, Experian, and TransUnion, have decided to report Chapter 13 bankruptcies for just seven years.

A Walk Through the Chapter 13 Process

Prior to filing for Chapter 13 your bankruptcy attorney will prepare your debt reorganization plan. The plan will describe what you intend to do about each of your debts. Among other things, it will indicate how much you plan on paying your creditors during the three to five years that the plan will be in effect. For example, if you have been having trouble keeping up with your car loan, the plan will explain how you intend to pay it so that you can keep the car. The bankruptcy court must approve your plan.

When your attorney is preparing your plan, she is legally obligated to deal with some debts before other debts, because the bankruptcy law views certain types of debts as more important than others. Therefore, she will tackle your priority debts first.

Those debts may include unpaid income and property taxes, past-due child support, and past-due spousal support. In a Chapter 13 bankruptcy, priority debts must be paid in full.

Next, your attorney will address your secured debts. There are several ways to deal with secured debt in a reorganization bankruptcy. For example, you can:

- Keep the collateral that secures the debt by paying what the collateral is worth plus interest over the length of your plan rather than what you owe on the debt. This arrangement can help you lower your payments on your car or furniture for example, especially if the asset has lost value since you financed its purchase. However, it does not apply to your homestead, which is the home that you have declared to be your legal residence. You must pay the full balance on your mortgage, not what your home is worth at the time that you file for bankruptcy.

- Give up your collateral so that you have one less debt to pay.

Watch Out!

Although you cannot use Chapter 13 to lower the amount of your monthly mortgage payments, you can use it to get three to five years to pay the past-due balance on your mortgage. However, during those years you must make all of your current mortgage payments on time.

Your attorney will deal with your unsecured debts last, including your credit card debt and any unsecured loans you may owe. These debts are the least important kind of debt in a bankruptcy, and, depending on your financial situation, you may end up paying little or nothing on them. However, federal bankruptcy law says that you must pay your unsecured creditors at least as much as they would receive if you had filed for Chapter 7. If you can't, the court will not approve your reorganization plan.

Thirty days after you file your reorganization plan, you will have to begin paying on your debts according to the terms of the plan. However, the plan may be changed later depending on the actions of your creditors and on the decisions of the bankruptcy judge. You will send your debt payments to the bankruptcy trustee who has been assigned to your case, not directly to your creditors. The trustee will receive and disburse your debt payments and will also monitor the progress of your bankruptcy.

Meanwhile, your attorney will contact your priority and secured creditors to find out if they have any problems with the way you are treating them in your plan and to try to resolve their objections prior to the date of your creditors' meeting. The meeting will occur 20–60 days after the start of your bankruptcy.

Any creditor who wants to can attend the creditors' meeting. However, your secured creditors are most apt to show up, because they will be concerned about what is going to happen to their collateral. During the meeting, your creditors, as well as the trustee assigned to your case, will ask you questions. Among other things, the trustee will want to be sure that you have been totally honest about your assets and debts, that you cannot pay more on your debts than the amounts you have indicated in your reorganization plan, and that you can live up to the terms of your reorganization plan.

Depending on the way your area's bankruptcy court works, a confirmation hearing will either take place the same day as the creditors' meeting or sometime later. At the hearing, the bankruptcy judge will hear any motions your creditors may make objecting to the approval of your reorganization plan. The judge will decide how to handle the objections, and in some instances the judge may ask you to revise your plan.

If the judge approves your plan, you must continue paying on your debts until you have completed the plan. Then the bankruptcy court will discharge or wipe out any debts that you may still owe except for any debts that cannot be discharged, and your bankruptcy will be over.

If the judge does not approve your plan, you and your attorney can go back to the "drawing board," revise it, and then try to get the judge to okay a new amended plan. However, if it does not look like you will ever get a reorganization plan approved, your lawyer will probably recommend that you petition the court to convert your Chapter 13 bankruptcy to a Chapter 7.

Living Up to Your Reorganization Plan

After your plan has been approved, if you realize that you are going to have trouble meeting its terms, get in touch with your attorney right away. Your attorney can file a motion with the court asking it to:

Watch Out!

If you convert to Chapter 7, you may have to give up the assets that you were trying to keep by filing Chapter 13.

- Reduce your debt payments for a limited period of time.

- Permanently change the terms of your reorganization plan. You might make this request if your finances have taken a turn for the worse and you do not expect things to turn around, but you want to continue paying on your debts.

- Convert your bankruptcy to a Chapter 7. The bankruptcy judge will not grant this motion if you have filed Chapter 7 within the previous six years.

- Grant you a hardship discharge. Your bankruptcy will end early if you get a hardship discharge, and the balance on the unsecured debts except the ones that you agreed to pay off over a three-to-five year period will be wiped out. The hardship discharge will not affect your obligation to pay your secured and priority debts, however. The court might grant this motion if a debilitating illness or injury or some other serious problem has made it impossible for you to continue paying on your debts. However, you will not be eligible for a hardship discharge unless you have paid the creditors in your reorganization plan at least as much as they would have received if you had filed for Chapter 7, and unless there is no possibility that with modifications you could continue paying your debts according to the plan.

Watch Out!

You can use Chapter 7 to delay, but not stop, a foreclosure or repossession.

Chapter 7 Bankruptcy

Chapter 7 is appropriate when you have so much debt relative to your income that you cannot afford to pay what you owe. After you file, the bankruptcy court will take your nonexempt assets, sell them, and use the sale proceeds to pay as much as possible on your debts, starting with your priority debts. In most

Chapter 7 bankruptcies, unsecured creditors end up receiving little or nothing of what they are owed.

Some of your debts may survive a Chapter 7 bankruptcy and you will have to pay them once the bankruptcy is over. Examples of these debts include your mortgage, your car loan, any past-due child support and/or alimony you may owe, student loans, most taxes, government penalties and fines, criminal penalties, and any debts that were not listed on your bankruptcy paperwork when your bankruptcy petition was filed. From start to finish, a Chapter 7 bankruptcy should take about six months.

After your Chapter 7 bankruptcy is over you can file Chapter 13 to get three-to-five years to pay off the debts you still owe.

A Walk Through the Chapter 7 Process

Before you file a Chapter 7 bankruptcy petition with the court, you will have some important decisions to make in consultation with your attorney. Among other things, you must decide:

- Which assets you want to exempt from your bankruptcy. If you are behind on your payments for any of these assets, your lawyer will contact the appropriate creditors and try to negotiate a way for you to catch up on the payments. If you are current on your payments on a collateralized debt and you want to keep the collateral, continue paying on it during your bankruptcy. Be sure to exempt every asset you are legally entitled to.

Watch Out!

Every time your attorney files a motion with the court, it will cost you more in attorney's fees and expenses.

● Whether to keep any nonexempt assets. You must get the bankruptcy trustee's permission to keep a nonexempt asset, but most likely, if the asset is worth a lot, he will not let you hold on to the asset because he will want to sell it and use the money to pay your creditors. You have two options if you owe money on a nonexempt asset that you want to keep and the trustee gives you permission to hold on to it. One option is for you and the creditor to agree on a plan for how you will get caught up on what you owe. The other option is to pay the value of the asset you want to keep. You and the creditor will have to agree on the value. If you can't agree, you can file a "Motion to Redeem" with the court, after which there will be a hearing. At the end of the hearing, the bankruptcy judge will tell you how much to pay. You will have to pay this amount in a lump sum and you will not have much time to pay it.

● Whether you want to reaffirm any of your secured debts. If you want to reaffirm a secured debt and the creditor that is associated with that debt has no objections to the reaffirmation, both of you will sign a reaffirmation agreement. When you do, you will agree to continue paying on the debt and the creditor will promise not to take back the asset that secures the debt as long as you keep up with the payments. If you do not live up to the terms of the reaffirmation agreement, the creditor can take the asset back once your bankruptcy is over and sell it. If the asset sells for less than what you owe on it, you will have to pay the deficiency. If you change your mind about reaffirming a debt within 60 days of signing a reaffirmation agreement, you can cancel the agreement and give the asset back to your creditor.

The creditors' meeting in your Chapter 7 bankruptcy will take place six-to-eight weeks after you file your bankruptcy petition. Like the creditors' meeting in a Chapter 13 bankruptcy any of your creditors can attend the meeting, but your secured creditors are most apt to show up. During the meeting, your creditors may ask you questions about how you plan to deal with your debts. If they don't like your answers and if your lawyer can't satisfy their concerns, they may file motions with the court to get back their collateral. There will be a hearing to consider the creditors' motions and the bankruptcy judge will decide what to do.

Watch Out!

If you lie about your assets or debts you could be prosecuted for bankruptcy fraud. However, if you realize that you left an asset or a debt off of your bankruptcy schedules when you filed them with the court, let the trustee know what happened. You made an honest mistake and you will not be penalized.

During your creditors' meeting, the trustee will ask you a series of questions about your financial affairs. Among other things, the trustee may question you about the completeness and accuracy of your bankruptcy paperwork as well as questions to help him feel confident that you are not hiding any nonexempt assets from the court.

Your attorney will prepare you for the trustee's questions, but to give you a head start, here are examples of the kinds of questions you will be asked:

- Why did you file for bankruptcy?

- Are your asset and debt schedules accurate and complete?

- How did you determine the value of your assets? The

trustee wants to make sure that you did not undervalue your assets. If he thinks you have, the trustee may hire an independent appraiser to value them.

● Do you expect to receive a tax refund? The trustee will want you to list the refund on your schedule of assets. If you are not able to exempt the refund, you may have to give it to the trustee.

● Are you entitled to damages as a result of an accident? If you are, the claim should be listed on your asset schedule.

● Do you expect to receive an inheritance within the next six months? The amount of the inheritance should be reflected on your schedule of assets. However, you may be able to exempt the inheritance from your bankruptcy.

Your creditors will have 60 days to object to the discharge of your debts after the creditors' meeting. If there are objections they will be heard at a court hearing and a bankruptcy judge will decide what to do about them.

The End of Your Bankruptcy

A discharge hearing on your Chapter 7 bankruptcy will take place 80-to-120 days after the creditor's meeting. Depending on the policies of the court that is in charge of your bankruptcy, you may not have to attend the hearing.

At the hearing, all of the debts you owe, other than the ones that you have reaffirmed and any debts that cannot be discharged, will be wiped out. At the end of the hearing, your Chapter 7 bankruptcy will be over.

Once you receive your discharge order, keep it in your home safe, bank safe-deposit box, or some other safe place. Should any of your creditors contact you in the future about a debt that was discharged, it will prove that you do not owe them money anymore.

After you receive your discharge order, send a copy of that document together with a copy of the debt schedules that were filed with the court at the start of your bankruptcy and a cover letter to each of the three national credit bureaus (Equifax, Experian, and TransUnion). The letter should ask each of the credit bureaus to update your credit record by indicating that the particular debts on the order have been discharged. Having this information in your credit record will be helpful once you are ready to begin the credit rebuilding process. Chapter 8 explains how credit bureaus work, tells you how to contact them, and explains the importance of having a good credit record. Chapter 9 tells how to rebuild your credit once your financial troubles are over.

LOOKING TOWARD A BRIGHTER FUTURE

8

CREDIT RECORD

BASICS

Your credit record is your financial report card. It provides a detailed history of how you manage your credit. A good credit record opens doors. A bad credit record— one that shows that you have been late paying your creditors, had accounts turned over to collections, defaulted on loans, lost your home in a foreclosure, and so on—does just the opposite. A credit record full of negatives will make it difficult, if not impossible, for you to borrow money at reasonable terms, to buy a home, rent an apartment, purchase adequate insurance, and even qualify for a job with responsibility for handling a lot of money.

Right now, because of your financial situation, the information in your credit record may be more negative than positive. However, once your money troubles are over, you can begin rebuilding your credit record, and eventually you will have a positive credit record again. But first, before you begin the rebuilding process, you should review your credit record so that you know what it says about you, and you should educate yourself about your credit record rights. That information is essential to the credit-rebuilding process and to maintaining a problem-free credit record in the future.

This chapter tells you how to order a copy of your credit record, reviews the kinds of information you will find in it, and tells you how to correct any errors in your credit record. It also explains how credit bureaus work, educates you about your credit record rights according to the federal Fair Credit Reporting Act (FCRA), and provides an overview of the information you will find in your credit record.

Credit Bureaus: The Keepers of Your Credit Record

Three national credit bureaus, Equifax, Experian, and Trans-Union, collect information on you and on nearly every consumer in this country. They maintain this information in vast, computerized databases. Your information is called a credit record, credit file, or credit history. A printed or on-line version of the information is called a credit report.

Credit bureaus sell their information to credit card companies, banks, mortgage lenders, and to other financial institutions, as well as to retailers, employers, insurance companies, large apartment leasing companies, and so on. In turn, those companies use the information to help them make decisions related to individual consumers, including you.

The information in your credit record comes from four key sources:

● *You.* The identifying information you provide when you apply for credit becomes a part of your credit record. That information includes your name and address, marital status, employer, and Social Security number.

● *Credit bureau subscribers.* Creditors and other companies provide the three national credit bureaus with information about your credit accounts and with other financial data on a regular or a periodic basis.

● *Collection agencies.* Some collection agencies report to the national credit bureaus when they are trying to collect on a consumer debt.

● *Public records.* Credit bureaus get information about bankruptcies, tax liens, foreclosures, court judgments, and so on, from court records.

The federal Fair Credit Reporting Act (FCRA) regulates credit bureaus and gives you specific rights when it comes to your credit record. Those rights include the right to obtain a copy of your credit report and the right to have credit record errors corrected. Many states have their own laws that regulate credit bureaus.

What's in Your Credit Record

Your credit record contains four different categories of information:

● *Identifying information.* This information includes your name, current and most recent past address, your Social Security number, whether you are a senior, junior, II, III, et cetera, your date of birth, and the names of your current and past employers. If you are married, your credit record also contains identifying information for your spouse.

● *Information about your credit accounts.* For each account in your credit record, you will find among other things: the creditor's name, the account number and the type of account, the outstanding balance on the account, how often you have been late paying on the account, whether you have defaulted on the account, and whether the account has been turned over to collections or been closed by the creditor.

● *Inquiries.* This section of your credit report indicates who has taken a peek at your credit record information over the past two years. The inquiries may be there for one of several reasons:

- You applied for new or additional credit.
- One of your creditors reviewed your credit record information to help it decide whether or not to increase or decrease your credit limit, change the rate of interest on your account, or cancel your account. The letters *AM* (account monitoring) or *AR* (account review) appear next to these kinds of inquiries.
- A creditor reviewed your credit record to decide whether to offer you preapproved credit. This kind of inquiry is signified by the letters *PRM* (promotional).
- An employer, landlord, insurer, et cetera, took a gander at your credit record to help it make a decision related to you.
- You ordered a copy of your credit record.

- *Public record information.* Information in this section of your credit record comes from court records. It may reflect the bankruptcies that you filed over the past ten years (seven years for Chapter 13 bankruptcies), as well as the foreclosures, repossessions, outstanding court judgments and tax liens, and child-support delinquencies that are a part of your history.

The FCRA says that inquiries related to your employment must remain in your credit record for two years. All other types of inquiries must stay there for at least six months. However, the law does not say when the inquiries must be removed.

You have a right to ask a credit bureau for the address and phone number of any business or individual who shows up in your credit report as an inquiry. You must make the request in writing.

The information in your credit report will vary depending on which of the three national credit bureaus you order it from, because each credit bureau obtains its information from different subscribers. Therefore, it is advisable that you order a copy of your report from each of the three national credit bureaus.

When you review your credit report, you may be surprised to discover the amount of information that is not in it. For example, you may not find information about your mortgage payments unless you have been at least 90

Watch Out!

Having a lot of credit-related inquiries in your credit record that you have initiated can work against you when you apply for new or additional credit. Creditors may assume from all of the inquiries that you are either short of cash and need more credit to help pay your bills, or that you are taking on more debt that you can handle. Therefore, only apply for the credit that you *really* need.

days late with a payment or unless your home has been fore-closed on. Also, you will probably not find any payment history information related to your rent, utilities, or phone bill unless you have been sued for eviction, had an account sent to collections, or unless a creditor has a judgment lien against you. Other creditors who do not regularly report account payment information to credit bureaus include national and local retailers who extend credit to consumers and medical providers.

Most negative information stays in your credit record for seven years, but some information may stick around longer. For example:

● Chapter 7 bankruptcies can be reported for up to ten years.

● Information about a lawsuit or judgment against you can be reported for seven years or until the statute of limitations runs out—whichever is longer.

● Unpaid tax liens can be reported for as long as 15 years.

● Information reported because of an application for a job with a salary of more than $75,000 or for more than $150,000 worth of credit or life insurance has no time limitation.

Who Can Take a Peek at Your Credit Record Information

The FCRA limits who can find out what your credit record says about you. It says that only the following can take a gander at your credit record information:

● *Creditors.* They can review the information to help them decide whether or not to give you new or additional credit, whether they should cancel your account, and whether they should change the terms of your existing credit.

● *Government agencies.* The government can use your credit record information when they are deciding whether or not to give you a professional license or a security clearance, and to help them determine if you are eligible to receive certain government benefits. Also, if you are not paying your court-ordered child support, the government office responsible for making you pay up can review your credit record as part of its collection effort.

● *Insurance companies.* They can review your credit history as part of their decision-making process when you apply for new or additional coverage.

● *Employers.* Your current employer or a prospective employer can read the information in your credit record to help decide whether or not to hire or promote you, but you must give them written permission to look at that information first.

● Anyone to whom you give written permission.

● Anyone who has a "legitimate business need" to review your credit file.

How to Obtain a Copy of Your Credit Record

The FCRA gives you the right to obtain a copy of your own credit report and to have the credit bureau that produced it correct any errors and inaccuracies you may find in it. Don't forget, the information in your credit record will vary somewhat from credit bureau to credit bureau, so order a copy of your report from each of the three national credit bureaus. Review all three when you are applying for credit, insurance, a place to rent, or for a new job or a promotion, because you will not know ahead of time which of your credit reports will be reviewed—the one produced by Equifax, Experian, or TransUnion—and, you should make certain that the information in all three of your credit reports is accurate.

With some exceptions, you will have to pay an up-front fee and the applicable state sales tax to obtain your credit record information. The fee will range from $2 to $10 depending on your state. However, in some states you can obtain a free, annual copy of your report. Also, you are entitled to a free copy of your credit report if you have been turned down for credit, insurance, employment, or rental housing during the previous 60 days because of information in the report. The company that turned you down is legally obligated to provide you with the name, address, and phone number of the credit bureau that supplied it with the information.

Money$ense

Be prepared to pay for your credit report with a MasterCard or Visa when you order your credit report on-line or over the phone. If you don't have one, mail in your request and include a check for the cost of the report.

The process for ordering a copy of your credit report varies from credit bureau to credit bureau. You may be able to order a copy of your report by phone, using an interactive voice response system, through the mail, or on-line. The ordering options that apply to you will depend on the credit bureau you are ordering from, your state, and on why you are ordering a copy of your credit report. For the most up-to-date ordering instructions as well as specific credit report cost information, call the following toll-free numbers: (These are also the phone numbers you would call to order a copy of your credit reports over the telephone.)

- Equifax: 1-800-685-1111

- Experian: 1-888-397-3742

- TransUnion: 1-800-888-4213

If you want to order a copy of your credit reports on-line, go to these Web sites:

- Equifax: www.econsumer.equifax.com

- Experian: www.experian.com

- TransUnion: www.transunion.com

Each of these sites also provides general information about credit reports, correcting errors, et cetera.

Ordering by Mail

You must provide very specific information when you request a copy of your credit report through the mail. The information helps a credit bureau locate you in its database and also helps it make sure that you are who you say you are—the credit bureau does not want to give your credit record information to someone who is pretending to be you. If your letter does not provide all of the required information, your request will not be processed.

Therefore, be sure to include the following information in your credit report request letter:

- Your full name, including middle name and whether you are a junior, senior, a II, III, and so on.

- Your Social Security number.

- Your date of birth.

- Your phone number including area code.

- Your current address as well as any other addresses at which you may have resided over the past five years. Include all applicable apartment numbers and zip codes.

- Your spouse's full name, assuming you are married.

- The name of your current employer.

In addition, if you are ordering a copy of your Equifax credit report and you have moved during the last six months, attach two different proofs of your current address to your letter. Copies of your driver's license, bank statement, telephone or utility bills are all legitimate proofs of residence. Be sure to sign the letter and enclose a check or money order in the appropriate amount. Send your letters to:

- Equifax
  PO Box 105873
  Atlanta, GA 30348

- Experian
  National Consumer Assistance Center
  PO Box 2104
  Allen, TX 75013–2104

- Trans Union
  Consumer Disclosure Center
  PO Box 1000
  Chester, PA 19022

You should receive a copy of your credit report within eight-to-ten days after the credit bureau receives your request.

Correcting Credit Record Errors

Review your credit report carefully so you can be sure that all of the information in it is accurate. The FCRA gives you the right to have inaccurate credit record information corrected or deleted. However, only time makes negative but true information go away.

If you find an error in your credit report, ask the credit bureau that produced the report to conduct an investigation. Make this request by following the specific instructions that will come with the report. You may be directed to call a specific phone number or to fill out the "research request" or "investigation request" form that may have come with the report.

If you complete a research request or investigation request form, mail it back to the return address on the form. Send it via certified mail, return receipt requested. If you need more writing space than the form provides, use a separate piece of paper and attach it to the form. Also, if you have information that helps prove the error you are writing about, attach copies of the information to the form. The information might include receipts, canceled checks, letters, and so on. Make a copy of your completed form and file it with the supporting information.

Common Credit Record Problems

Stay alert for problems when you review your credit record. The ones that follow represent many of the most common types of credit record errors:

• Your credit record includes information that does not belong to you.

• Information is commingled. Commingled information is information that belongs to someone with a name that is similar or identical to yours.

• Your name is misspelled; your generation is inaccurate—you are shown as a junior when you are a senior, for example; your address is incorrect or outdated; your Social Security number is wrong.

• Incorrect account numbers.

• Inaccurate or incomplete account information. For example, your credit record does not show that you paid off an account balance, that you closed an account, or that a tax lien was released. Or, it incorrectly shows that you were late with a payment or that an account was sent to collections.

• Negative information that should no longer be reported is still a part of your credit record. An earlier section of this chapter, What's in Your Credit Record, indicates how long different kinds of information can stay in your credit record.

The Investigation Process

The FCRA says that once a credit bureau receives your investigation request letter, it must do certain things within certain periods of time. First, within five days of receiving your investigation request the credit bureau must contact the business or government agency that supplied it with the information you are disputing to confirm or deny its accuracy.

If the error is confirmed the credit bureau must correct your credit record immediately. It must also let the other two national credit bureaus know about the correction so that they can change their own records as necessary.

If a credit bureau believes that your investigation request is frivolous, it has a legal right to refuse to investigate. However, it must notify you in writing of its refusal and it must tell you why it thinks that your request has no merit. If you disagree with the credit bureau's decision, try to locate information that can help you prove there is a legitimate reason to conduct an investigation. If you do, and the credit bureau continues to balk, talk with a consumer law attorney who has experience dealing with credit bureaus. You may have the basis for a lawsuit.

Whatever the outcome of the credit bureau's investigation, it must inform you in writing of its findings within five days of completing the investigation. If the credit bureau concludes that there is an error in your credit record, it must send you:

- A revised copy of your credit record reflecting the change or deletion that it made to correct the error.

- A notice that upon request it will provide you with a description of the procedure it used to research the accuracy of your credit record information, including the names, addresses, and phone numbers, "if reasonably available" of the creditors it contacted as part of its research.

● A notice that you have the right to ask the credit bureau to send a copy of your corrected credit report to any employer who reviewed your credit record information over the past two years and to anyone else who may have reviewed it over the past 6 months (12 months for residents of Maryland, New York, and Vermont). However, you must provide the credit bureau with the names and addresses of those who should receive a copy. You may also have to pay the credit bureau a fee for each credit report it sends out.

Order another copy of your credit report a couple of months after the credit bureau corrects any problems you found in it so you can be sure that the error has not returned. Sometimes information that you thought had been deleted or corrected shows up again due to computer or human error.

If a credit bureau concludes that everything in your credit record is accurate, it must send you a notice to that effect. It must also send you:

Money$ense

If you ask a credit bureau to mail a corrected copy of your credit report to a creditor or to someone else, ask it to provide you with written confirmation that the report was sent.

● A notice that if you disagree with the outcome of its investigation you have the right to prepare a written statement of not more than 100 words explaining why you think your credit record is inaccurate. The credit bureau must make the statement a part of your credit record. If you need help preparing your statement, call the credit bureau. It is legally obligated to help you.

● A notice that you have the right to ask for a written description of the procedure the credit bureau used to conduct its investigation, including the names, addresses, and the phone numbers, "if reasonably available," of whomever it contacted during the investigation.

Watch Out!

The value of written statements is diminishing because a growing number of creditors and others are using consumer credit scores in their decision-making process rather than reviewing consumer credit records. Your credit score is a numerical representation of your credit worthiness and is derived in part from your credit record information. You can learn more about credit scores by reading the section of this chapter called Do You Know the Score?

Other Things You Can Do When You Disagree with the Outcome of an Investigation

Aside from writing a statement, there are other things that you can do when you disagree with the outcome of a credit bureau's investigation. For example you can:

● Find additional information that helps prove the error and send copies of the information to the credit bureau.

● Contact whoever provided the credit bureau with the incorrect information to try to verify the error with it. If you confirm the error, ask the business or agency you contacted to provide the credit bureau with corrected information, and a couple of weeks later follow up with the credit bureau yourself to make sure that the correction was received. Then, a month or two after that, order another copy of your credit record to verify that it has been corrected.

● Hire an attorney to sue the credit bureau and/or the organization that supplied it with the incorrect information. The FCRA gives you the right to file a lawsuit in either federal or state court when your credit record rights have been violated. You can sue for actual as well as punitive damages, and if you win your lawsuit, you can collect attorney's fees and court costs. When you are looking for legal help, be sure to hire a consumer law attorney with specific experience representing clients in lawsuits related to credit records and credit bureaus. If you have a strong case, the attorney may take your case on a contingent-fee basis. Chapter 6 provided the names of two organizations you can contact for referrals to consumer law attorneys in your area.

Watch Out!

Lawsuits against credit bureaus and their information providers are very difficult to win.

● File a complaint with the Federal Trade Commission (FTC) and with your state attorney general's office if your state has its own law regulating credit bureaus.

Do You Know the Score?

A growing number of creditors, insurance companies, employers, and so on are using credit scores rather than actual credit reports to make decisions about consumers. Your credit score is derived from the information in your credit record, although it may take other information into account as well, including whether or not you are a home owner, your occupation, and how long you have had a credit record. Credit scores range from 300 to 900. The higher the score, the better.

Each of the national credit bureaus calculates consumer credit scores using software developed by Fair, Isaac and Company. As a result, their credit scores are commonly referred to as FICO scores. Your score will vary from credit bureau to credit bureau, since the information one credit bureau has on you usually differs somewhat from the information the other two companies have in their files.

You can learn your FICO score by going to *www.myfico.com* or by ordering it directly from the three credit bureaus. You may have to pay as much as $12.95 to get your score.

To order from the credit bureaus, call the following numbers:

- Equifax: 1-800-685-1111

- Experian: 1-800-397-3742

- TransUnion: 1-800-916-8800

Tips for Boosting Your Credit Score

You can raise your credit score by doing, or not doing, certain things. Not surprisingly, these things will also help you maintain a positive credit record and will help keep you out of financial trouble. Your credit score will go up if you:

● Keep the outstanding balances on your credit cards to a minimum.

● Avoid taking on a lot of debt relative to your income.

● Don't have a lot of open credit accounts.

● Minimize the number of credit cards you have.

● Pay your debts on time. Being late, having accounts in collection, and filing for bankruptcy will lower your credit score.

● Make sure that all of the information in your credit record is accurate.

● Don't make a habit of transferring credit card balances from one credit card to another. An occasional transfer is okay.

● Avoid finance company loans.

9

LOOKING TO THE FUTURE: HOW TO REBUILD YOUR CREDIT

Credit is the lifeblood of our society. Without credit or without adequate credit at reasonable terms, it will be difficult if not impossible for you to buy a home, send your kids to college, or take a nice vacation, among other things. Therefore, if your money troubles have damaged your credit record, your financial future may not seem especially bright right now, and accomplishing relatively simple transactions like renting a car, reserving a hotel room, and purchasing items on-line may be complicated.

Once your money troubles are over, however, you can rebuild your credit record so that once again you can have access to credit with attractive terms. Therefore, this chapter takes you through the credit-rebuilding process, including applying for a secured MasterCard or Visa and for a secured and an unsecured bank loan. It also explains how credit-repair firms work, what your legal rights are if you decide to work with one, and how to spot a bogus credit fix-it firm.

An Overview of the Rebuilding Process

Rebuilding your credit history is all about demonstrating to creditors that your money problems are over and that you can manage new credit responsibly. There is no secret formula for how to prove this. It is simply a matter of applying for a small amount of credit from a reputable lender, paying off that debt according to the terms of your credit agreement, getting a little more credit, paying that debt off the same way, and so on. Gradually, by following this process, your credit record will begin to include more and more positive information. At the same time, the negative information in your credit record that is the result of your money troubles will eventually go away because, as you learned in the previous chapter, most negative information cannot stay in your credit record for longer than seven years.

You can start the credit-rebuilding process as soon as your money troubles are over and you are financially stable again. However, the credit that you obtain initially will probably come with less favorable terms than if your credit record was problem free. In addition, depending on how serious your money problems were, you may not be able to qualify for a traditional unsecured MasterCard or Visa card right away and may have to apply for a secured credit card instead. The section of this chapter titled Start With a Credit Card discusses how secured credit cards work.

If your money troubles damaged but did not ruin your credit history and you still have access to credit and have been making on-time payments on those accounts for a while, write to each of your creditors. Explain why you got behind on your account, call attention to your recent payment history, and ask that they remove the negative account information from your credit record. If the reason or reasons for your credit problems were beyond your control—you were laid off from your job for example—your creditors may be willing to comply with your request. Whenever a creditor agrees to get rid of negative credit record information, draft a written agreement and send it to the creditor, certified mail, return receipt requested, for the creditor to sign. Assuming the creditor does, check your credit record a couple of months later to make sure that the creditor followed through.

Eventually, once all of the negative information is gone and assuming you make timely payments on all of your new credit accounts and don't do anything else to damage your credit record, you will have an A+ credit record. Then, you and your family will be able to benefit from all of the opportunities that having a good credit record can bring.

A new, problem-free credit record won't happen overnight. It will take years for the negative information to go away and it will take a couple of years at least to build a new track record of responsible credit management for yourself. Like the tortoise in the parable of the tortoise and the hare, a slow and steady pace will get you where you want to go. You may get frustrated at times, but do not try to shorten the rebuilding process by working with a credit-repair or debt-counseling firm that promises to speed things up by making the negative information in your credit record disappear. They use illegal techniques. The section in this chapter titled Bogus Credit Fix-it Firms explains how these companies work.

Getting Ready to Rebuild

A savings account is the foundation of the credit-rebuilding process. You will need money in savings to get a loan, and if you cannot qualify for an unsecured credit card right away, you will need money in savings to qualify for a secured credit card.

Money$ense

An easy way to build up your savings is to have your employer direct deposit money into your account each month. If you never have the money, you won't miss it or be tempted to spend it before you can get it into your savings account.

Start building up your savings account as soon as you can afford to by making regular contributions to that account. How much you save is less important than how often you save—consistency is key to a successful savings program.

Order a copy of your credit report from each of the three national credit bureaus. Review each of the reports for errors, and correct any problems you may find. The errors can interfere with your rebuilding efforts. Chapter 8 explains how to order a copy of your credit report and how to correct errors.

If you have accounts in good standing that are not a part of your credit history, write to each of the national credit bureaus to ask that they add information about those accounts to your credit record. Attach to your letters a copy of your most recent account statements as well as a history of your account payments. Although credit bureaus are not legally obligated to comply with your request, if one does, having that information in your credit record will help you achieve your rebuilding goal.

Once you have at least $1,000 in your savings account and have corrected any problems in your credit record, apply first for a Visa or MasterCard. Then, apply for a small bank loan.

Start with a Credit Card

If credit cards helped create your financial problems, it might be better if you never had one again. However, doing without a major credit card in today's society makes life difficult. Therefore, start the credit-rebuilding process by applying for a MasterCard or Visa. Shop for the card with the best terms of credit. Chapter 2 explains how to compare cards.

If you can't qualify for an unsecured MasterCard or Visa with reasonable terms of credit right away, apply for a secured MasterCard or Visa instead. Then, once you have established a good payment history with the secured card, you can apply for an unsecured card.

A secured credit card and an unsecured credit card look exactly the same and you use them the same way. The main difference between the two cards is that you have to collateralize the purchases you make using a secured card by opening a savings account with the card issuer or by purchasing a Certificate of Deposit (CD) from that bank. You will not have access to the collateral.

When you have a secured credit card, you can charge up to a percentage of the value of your collateral—usually between 50 and 100 percent. If you fall behind on your credit card payments, the issuer will send your account directly to collections or take a portion of your collateral as payment, depending on what your credit card agreement says. Also, if your account is closed with an outstanding balance, the issuer will take as much of the collateral as it needs to pay off the balance.

Most secured cards come with very low initial credit limits, just $500 in many instances. However, once you establish a good payment history on the card, the card issuer may be willing to increase your credit limit. To get the increase you may have to increase your collateral too.

Some secured credit cards have better terms of credit than others, just like regular credit cards do. Therefore, when you are in the market for a secured card, shop around for the best deal. However, there are additional criteria to consider when you are in the market for a secured card.

Savvy Advice for Secure Card Shopping

When you are in the market for a secured credit card and want to get the best deal, you have more criteria to take into account than if you are shopping for an unsecured credit card. Here is a rundown on the most important criteria to consider when you compare secured credit card offers:

• How much you have to pay to apply for the card.

• Whether you can get your application fee back if you are turned down for the card.

• Whether there are other fees associated with the card and the amount and the nature of those fees.

• The amount of money you must put up as collateral.

• The rate of interest you will earn on the collateral. You want to earn as much as possible.

• The size of your credit limit.

• The interest rate on the card.

• Whether you can increase the credit limit. If you can, note how long you must wait to ask for an increase, whether or not you have to put up additional collateral to get an increase, and any other conditions that may apply to the increase.

• Whether the card has a grace period and the length of the grace period.

• When the credit card company is entitled to draw on your collateral.

• Whether you can convert the secured card to an unsecured card. If you can, be clear about the terms and conditions of the conversion—how long you must wait to convert, whether you must pay a conversion fee, the rate of interest on the unsecured card, and so on.

• Whether you have to pay a fee if you or the card issuer closes the account.

• How quickly you can get your collateral back, assuming you are entitled to it after your account is closed, and under what-conditions the card issuer can keep all or some of the collateral.

Be sure that the issuer of a secured card will report your payment history to at least one, but preferably all three, of the national credit bureaus. Otherwise, having the card will not help you achieve your goal of creating a new positive credit history for yourself. Also, secured credit cards issued by companies that do not report to any of the national credit bureaus tend to come with very poor terms of credit.

Once you have a secured credit card, use it to either purchase a big ticket item you really need and then pay the balance off over time, or use it to make small purchases and pay the balance in full each month. Either of these strategies will help you begin building a positive new credit history for yourself, assuming you make your payments on time.

Money$ense

Use *www.bankrate.com* to shop for a secured credit card. It provides the names and contact information for various secured credit card issuers and summarizes the most important terms of credit for each card.

Watch Out!

Avoid secured credit card companies that make big promises in their advertising. They tend to come with high application fees, high interest rates, and other unattractive terms of credit. Some secured credit card companies will take your application fee but never give you a credit card. Others will send you a list of banks that issue secured cards in return for your application fee, or will issue you a credit card that you can only use to purchase items from a special catalog.

Get a Loan

Getting a loan is the next step in the credit-rebuilding process. Therefore, once you have between $500 and $1,000 in your savings account—this is in addition to the money that is securing your credit card—call the bank or credit union where the account is located and speak with a loan officer. If you already have a loan officer, call him. Explain that you are rebuilding your credit record after money troubles and that as part of the process, you would like to get a loan. In general terms, tell the loan officer what led to your money troubles and let him know what you have done to turn your finances around.

If the loan officer says that applying for a loan right now is a waste of your time, or if you are turned down for a loan after completing a loan application, contact another lender. If you can't find a bank or credit union willing to loan you money, keep saving and keep using your secured credit card responsibly. Eventually as your financial situation improves and once your credit record begins to show a history of timely credit card payments you will be able to qualify for a loan. It may just take longer than you had hoped it would.

> **Money$ense**
>
> Scheduling a face-to-face meeting with a loan officer may increase your chances of getting the loan you want. It is harder to say no to someone who is sitting across from you.

Once you get a loan, it will probably be a short-term secured loan for a relatively small amount of money—between $500 and $1,000. Be sure to make all of your payments on time so that the loan helps rebuild your credit. Late payments and missed payments will do just the opposite.

Apply for a Second Loan

Once you have paid your loan off, apply for a second loan. You can apply to the same bank or credit union that gave you the first loan, or you can apply to another financial institution. Shop for the best deal. This time, you may be able to qualify for a small unsecured loan. If you cannot, apply for a second secured loan. Assuming you meet all of your credit obligations, you will qualify for an unsecured loan eventually.

Before you apply for a second loan, order a copy of your credit report from whichever credit bureau or bureaus the first lender reports to. Check to make sure that it accurately reflects your loan payment history. If your payment history information is not there, contact the lender to find out why it did not report your payments and ask the lender to report them. If there are any errors in your credit report, follow the process outlined in the previous chapter to correct them. Don't apply for additional credit until you have cleared up the problems.

Bogus Credit Fix-It Firms

If you do not feel comfortable doing your own credit rebuilding and you want professional help, be careful whom you work with. Avoid businesses that claim they can clean up your credit record fast or make negative credit record information—even bankruptcies—magically disappear. Their credit-rebuilding methods may violate federal law as well as the laws in some states, and if you give them your money, you may be violating the law too.

Check out the credit repair firm you are thinking about using with your local Better Business Bureau, your state attorney general's office of consumer protection, and with the Federal Trade Commission. Also, don't work with a firm that asks you to do anything illegal or that gives you a money-back guarantee. Although the guarantee may sound attractive, the firm is apt to take your money and run.

One of the more common illegal methods used by bogus credit repair firms is called *file segregation* or *skin shedding,* which involves fooling creditors into thinking that you are someone else—someone without a damaged credit history. Firms that use this technique will tell you to apply to the federal government for an Employer Identification Number (EIN) and then to use that number rather than your Social Security number whenever you apply for new credit. They may also tell you to put a new address on each of your credit applications and suggest other ways of falsifying your credit applications.

Other firms that promise to help you rebuild your credit may not use illegal techniques, but they may charge substantial fees for their services. Paying those fees is a waste of your money since credit repair firms cannot do anything that you cannot do for yourself for little or no money. Rebuilding your credit is not difficult to do and you do not need professional help to do it.

Credit-repair firms have been such a big problem for consumers that the federal government passed the Credit Repair Organizations Act (CROA) to regulate them and to help protect consumers. Among other things, the CROA says that a credit repair firm:

- Must give you a written contract that spells out the services it will provide to you as well as the total cost of those services.

- Must provide you with a copy of "Your Consumer Credit File Rights Under State and Federal Law" before you sign a contract with it. This information tells you that you are legally entitled to obtain a copy of your own credit record and to get any inaccurate or out-of-date information corrected.

- Must tell you that you have a right to cancel your contract with the firm within three days of signing it. The firm should give you a special cancellation form when you sign the contract.

- Cannot take any money from you until it has completed all of the services spelled out in your contract.

If you sign a contract with a credit repair firm and the firm violates the CROA, the contract will be null and void—as though you never signed it. You will not be obligated to pay the firm any money for its services, even if it did everything in your contract.

You can also sue the firm in federal court for actual damages or for the money you paid to the company—whichever is greater—as well as for punitive damages. Punitive damages are intended to punish the firm for violating the law and to discourage it from breaking the law again.

Don't try to handle the lawsuit yourself. Hire a consumer law attorney who has filed similar lawsuits in the past. Assuming you have a strong case, the attorney will probably take your case on a contingent-fee basis. If you win your lawsuit, the credit repair firm must reimburse you for your expenses and for your attorney's fees.

Money$ense

If your state has its own credit-repair law, your attorney may sue using that law rather than the CROA. He will make that decision based on the facts of your case and on which law provides you with the opportunity for the biggest judgment.

Some Final Words of Advice

When your money troubles are over, don't try to get a lot of credit. You risk repeating the very same mistakes that damaged your credit record the first time. Furthermore, every time you apply for credit, it will show up on your credit record as an inquiry, and a lot of inquiries will undercut your credit-record rebuilding efforts.

Once you have a new, positive credit record, continue living on a budget, saving regularly, and try to live on a cash-only basis as much as possible. If you want something and you don't have the money for it, don't pay for the purchase with a credit card; save to buy it. When you do use a credit card, always try to pay off the full amount of your card balance before you purchase anything else with it.

APPENDIX

This appendix refers you to books, nonprofit organizations, government agencies, and Web sites that you can turn to for help and information.

Maintaining a Healthy Relationship with Money

HELPFUL ORGANIZATIONS

Debtors Anonymous. This nonprofit organization helps consumers overcome their spending problems using the proven techniques of Alcoholics Anonymous. It has chapters across the country.

To get the address and phone number of Debtors Anonymous chapters in various cities around the country and to learn more about the Debtors Anonymous Organization, go to *www.debtorsanonymous.org*. You can also call 1-781-453-2743, or write to the organization at: General Service Office, PO Box 920888, Needham, MA 02492-0009.

BOOKS ABOUT THE ROLE OF MONEY IN YOUR LIFE

The Money Trap: A Practical Program to Stop Self-Defeating Financial Habits so You Can Reclaim Your Grip on Life by Ron Gallen, Harper Resource, 2001.

Couples and Money: A Couples' Guide Updated for the New Millennium by Victoria Collins, Ph.D, Gabriel Books, 1998.

For Richer, Not Poorer: The Money Book for Couples by Ruth L. Hayden, Health Communications, Inc., 1999.

Money Harmony: Resolving Money Conflicts in Your Life and Your Relationships by Olivia Mellan, Walker & Co., 1995.

Living on Less

BOOKS ABOUT HOW TO SPEND LESS

Cheap Talk with the Frugal Friends: Over 600 Tips, Tricks, and Creative Ideas for Saving Money by Angie Zalewski, Deana Ricks, Starburst Publishers, 2001.

The Cheapskate Monthly Money Makeover by Mary Hunt, St. Martin's Press, 1995.

Get Clark Smart: The Ultimate Guide to Getting Rich From America's Money-Saving Expert by Clark Howard and Mark Meltzer, Hyperion Press, 2002.

How to Save Money Every Day by Ellie Kay, Bethany House, 2001.

Mary Hunt's Debt-Proof Living by Mary Hunt, Broadman & Holman Publishers, 1999.

50 Simple Things You Can Do to Improve Your Personal Finances: How to Spend Less, Save More and Make the Most of What You Have by Ilyce Glink, Three Rivers Press, 2001.

Making More Money

NONPROFIT ORGANIZATIONS AND WEB SITES

Bankrate.com's Small Biz Home Page (*www.bankrate.com*). This Web site provides basic information and advice about planning and financing a small business, including information about cash flow and banking, borrowing and e-commerce.

Bizymoms.com (*www.bizymoms.com*). Written for stay-at-home moms who want to combine running a home-based business with motherhood, this Web site provides advice about starting and running a business at home. It also offers an overview of various home-business opportunities and highlights business scams. *Home WorkingMom.com* (*www.homeworkingmom.com*) targets the same audience.

Business Owner's Toolkit (*www.toolkit.cch.com*). You can find downloadable checklists, model business plans, forms and documents, on-line small-business advice, and lots of helpful information on starting, running, and growing a small business at this Web site.

Business@Home (*www.gohome.com*). This is the on-line version of a publication called *Business at Home.*

Entrepreneur.com. (*www.entrepreneurmag.com*). This Web site not only provides a wide variety of business how-to information, but also offers in-depth information about legitimate business opportunities you may want to invest in, specific information for home-based businesses and e-businesses, an on-line version of the current issue of *Entrepreneur Magazine,* and a lot more.

Lycos Small Business Cannel (*www.business.lycos.com*). This is a comprehensive Web site for aspiring entrepreneurs as well as established small-business owners. The Web site features how-to articles, columns, and tools in the areas of entrepreneurship, finance, sales and marketing, and human resources. It also provides specific advice related to home-based and on-line businesses.

Service Corps of Retired Executives (SCORE). SCORE is a nonprofit organization dedicated to helping aspiring business owners as well as established small-business owners. It is made up of retired executives and business owners who donate their time and expertise to provide counseling and mentoring free of charge. For more information about how SCORE can help you, go to its Web site at *www.score.org.* You can also locate the SCORE office nearest you at this site.

The Small Business Administration. Contact the SBA if you are thinking about starting your own business or if you already have one up and running. It offers a wealth of information, services, financing assistance as well as education and training. Call the SBA at 1-800-827-5722 or visit its Web site at *www.sba.gov.*

BOOKS ABOUT MAKING MORE MONEY

The Harvard Entrepreneurs Club Guide to Starting Your Own Business by Poonam Sharma, John Wiley & Sons, 1999.

Keeping the Books: Basic Recordkeeping and Accounting for the Successful Small Business by Linda Pinson, Dearborn Trade, 2001.

The McGraw-Hill Guide to Starting Your Own Business: A Step-by-Step Blueprint for the First Time Entrepreneur by Stephen C. Harper, McGraw-Hill Professional Publishing, 1992.

Moonlighting: Earn a Second Income at Home by Jo Frohbieter-Mueller, Oasis Press, 1999.

Small Business Kit for Dummies, by Richard D. Harroch, Hungry Minds, Inc., 1998.

Start Your Own Business: The Only Start-Up Book You'll Ever Need by Rieva Lesonsky, Inc., Entrepreneur Media, 2001.

Starting on a Shoestring: Building a Business Without a Bankroll by Arnold S. Goldstein, Wiley Small Business Edition, 1995.

Steps to Small Business Start-Up: Everything You Need to Know to Turn Your Idea into a Successful Business by Linda Pinson and Jerry Jinnett, Dearborn Trade, 2001.

What No One Ever Tells You About Starting Your Own Business: Real Life Start-Up Advice from 101 Successful Entrepreneurs by Jan Norman, Upstart Publications, 1999.

Small Time Operator: How to Start Your Own Business, Keep Your Books, Pay Your Taxes, and Stay Out of Trouble by Bernard B. Kamoroff, Bell Springs Publishing, 2000.

BOOKS ABOUT FINDING A NEW JOB OR CHANGING CAREERS
Changing Careers for Dummies by Carol L. McClelland, Hungry Minds, Inc., 2001.

Cover Letter Magic by Wendy S. Enelow and Louise Kursmark, Jist Works, 2000.

e-Resumes: Everything You Need to Know About Using Electronic Resumes to Tap into Today's Hot Job Market by Susan Britton Whitcomb and Pat Kendall, McGraw-Hill Text, 2001.

Executive Job-Changing Workbook by John Lucht, Owlet, 1994.

Knock 'Em Dead by Martin Yate, Adams Media Corporation, 2002.

The Pathfinder: How to Choose or Change Your Career for a Lifetime of Satisfaction and Success by Nicholas Lore, Fireside, 1998.

The Resume Handbook: How to Write Outstanding Resumes and Cover Letters for Every Situation by Arthur D. Rosenberg and David V. Hizer, Adams Media Corporation, 1996.

Resumes in Cyberspace: Your Complete Guide to a Computerized Job Search by Pat Criscito, Barrons, 2001.

Rites of Passage at $100,000 to $1 Million: Your Insider's Lifetime Guide to Executive Job-Changing and Faster Career Progress in the 21st Century by John Lucht, Viceroy, 2000.

Switching Careers: Career Changers Tell How and Why They Did It. Learn How You Can Too by Robert K. Otterbourg, Kiplinger Books, 2001.

Where Do I Go From Here? An Inspirational Guide To Making Au-thentic Career and Life Choices by Kenneth C. Ruge, McGraw-Hill Professional Publishing, 1998.

Dealing with Debt and Managing Your Money

HELPFUL ORGANIZATIONS AND WEB SITES

Bankrate.com (www.bankrate.com). This Web sit offers lots of helpful information about credit cards, debt, and money management, as well as the current rates on various types of credit and information about the best secured and unsecured credit card deals. The site also features a variety of on-line calculators, including calculators to help you figure out how much it will cost to pay off a loan or your credit card debt and a calculator to help you compute the size of your monthly loan payments. You can also sign up for a free Bankrate newsletter at this Web site.

DebtSmart Magazine. This on-line magazine can help you manage your debt, deal with your creditors, make wise spending decisions and a lot more. You can find it at *www.debtsmart.com.*

National Association of Consumer Advocates (NACA). NACA is a non-profit association of attorneys and consumer advocates who are com-mitted to protecting consumers from unfair and abusive business practices and to representing consumers when they are victimized by such practices. They take on abusive or unfair lenders, credit card com-panies, credit bureaus, automobile sellers and debt collectors, among others. If you feel that you have been victimized by a business and want legal help, call NACA for a referral to a consumer law attorney that can help you. You can reach NACA in Washington, D.C. by calling 1-202-452-1989.

National Consumer Law Center (NCLC). The nonprofit NCLC is the nation's foremost advocate for low-income consumers. It helps consum-ers deal with financial and legal problems such as debt collection, utility termination, repossessions, payday loans, school loans, and more. The

NCLC will also help you locate a consumer lawyer in your area. To reach the NCLC, go to its Web site at *www.consumerlaw.org*, call the organization at 617-542-8010, or write to it at 77 Summer Street, 10th Floor, Boston, MA 02110.

National Foundation for Credit Counseling (NFCC). This nonprofit organization maintains a network of more than 1,300 debt-counseling offices that provide free or low-cost assistance to financially troubled consumers to help them avoid bankruptcy and take control of their finances. When you schedule an appointment at one of its debt-counseling offices, a debt counselor will assess your financial situation, discuss your options for dealing with your debts, and may negotiate new, more affordable debt payment plans with your creditors. To locate the NFCC-affiliated debt-counseling office closest to you, call 1-800-388-2227, or go to the NFCC Web site at *www.nfcc.org*.

Getting Out of Debt

BOOKS ABOUT GETTING OUT OF DEBT AND MONEY MANAGEMENT

Buy Life or Debt: A One-Week Plan for a Lifetime of Financial Freedom by Stacy Johnson, Ballantine Books, 2001.

Credit Card Debt: Reduce Your Financial Burden in Three Easy Steps, by Alexander Daskaloff, Avon, 1999.

Credit Card & Debt Management: A Step-By-Step How-To Guide for Organizing Debt and Saving Money on Interest Payments by Scott Bilker, Press One, 1996.

Debt-free by 30: Practical Advice for the Young, Broke & Upwardly Mobile by Jason Anthony and Karl Cluck, Plume, 2001.

How to Get Out of Debt, Stay Out of Debt and Live Prosperously by Jerrold Mundis, Bantam Books, 1990.

Slash Your Debt, Save Money and Secure Your Future by Gerri Detweiler, Marc Eisenson, and Nancy Castleman, Financial Literacy Center, 1999.

Your Legal Rights When You Owe Too Much by Gudrun Maria Nickel, Sphinx Publishing, 2001.

Surviving Debt: A Guide for Consumers by Jonathan Sheldon and Gary Klein, National Consumer Law Center, 1996.

OTHER PUBLICATIONS

Consumer Reports. When you are in the market for a vehicle, appliance, electronic items, or a computer, use *Consumer Report*'s unbiased product ratings to find the best deal. You can obtain the information online at *www.consumerreports.org,* by subscribing to *Consumer Reports Magazine*, or by reading the magazine for free at your local library. *Consumer Reports* also publishes books and buying guides.

Going Through a Bankruptcy

BANKRUPTCY-RELATED ORGANIZATIONS AND WEB SITES

The American Bankruptcy Institute (ABI). The ABI's Web site includes a feature called *Consumer Corner* at *www.abiworld.org/consumer.* Here you can link up with a debt counseling organization that can help you manage your debts and avoid bankruptcy, read helpful articles, learn all about bankruptcy, and locate a board-certified bankruptcy attorney, among other things.

BOOKS ABOUT BANKRUPTCY

The Bankruptcy Kit by John Ventura, Dearborn Trade, 1996.

Debt and Bankruptcy by Steven D. Strauss, W. W. Norton & Company, 1998.

Debt Free!: Your Guide to Personal Bankruptcy Without Shame by James P. Caher, John M. Caher, Henry Holt, 1996.

Understanding Your Credit Report & Rebuilding Your Credit

After Bankruptcy: Simple Steps to Rebuilding Your Credit and Your Life by Anne Whiteley, Solstice Publishing, 2001.

Bounce Back From Bankruptcy: A Step-by-Step Guide to Getting Back on Your Financial Feet by Paula Langguth Ryan, Pellingham Casper Communications, 2001.

Credit After Bankruptcy: A Step-By-Step Action Plan to Quick and Lasting Recovery after Personal Bankruptcy by Stephen Snyder, Bell-wether, 2001.

The Credit Repair Kit: Correct Errors in Your Credit Report, Rebuild Your Credit After Financial Troubles, Protect Your Legal Rights, Benefit from Recent Changes in the Law by John Ventura, Dearborn Trade, 1998.

The Guerrilla Guide to Credit Repair: How to Find Out What's Wrong With Your Credit Rating And How to Fix It by Todd Bierman and Nathaniel Wice, St. Martin's Press, 1994.

The Ultimate Credit Handbook by Gerri Detwieler, Plume, 1997.

General Nonprofit and Government Resources

Better Business Bureau. Contact your local Better Business Bureau (BBB) before you work with a business you are unfamiliar with. You can also check out a business by calling the National Council of Better Business Bureaus at 1-703-276-0100 or by visiting its Web site at *www.betterbusinessbureau.com.* The organization also publishes brochures about a variety of consumer-related topics and offers dispute resolution services.

Consumer Action Handbook. This invaluable publication is published by the Federal Consumer Information Center and is updated annually. It provides advice and consumer tips about how to use credit cards wisely, purchase or lease a car, get your car repaired, shop from home, steer clear of consumer and investment scams, finance home improvements, and resolve your own simple consumer problems, among other things. The handbook also includes a Consumer Assistance Directory which provides contact information for national consumer organizations, Better Business Bureaus, corporations, trade associations, state and local consumer protection offices, state agencies, military consumer offices, and federal agencies. You can read the handbook on-line or you can order a hard copy of the handbook at *www.pueblo.gsa.gov.* You can also order a copy by writing to: Consumer Information Center, PO Box 100, Pueblo, CO 81009.

Federal Consumer Information Center (FCIC). The FCIC offers many free and low-cost publications on a wide variety of consumer topics, including such topics as how to buy a used car, how to save money on insurance, credit and credit records, debt, preparing an effective resume, resources for finding a job, home equity loans and lines of credit, and much more. Go to *www.pueblo.gsa.gov* to read an on-line version of the *Consumer Information Catalog* and to order catalog publications. You can also order a copy of the catalog by writing to: Consumer Information Center, PO Box 100, Pueblo, CO 81009.

Federal Trade Commission (FTC). This government agency enforces a variety of consumer protection laws, including the Credit Repair Organizations Act, the Fair Credit Billing Act, the Fair Credit Reporting Act, the Fair Debt Collection Practices Act, the Home Equity Loan Consumer Protection Act, the Home Ownership and Equity Protection Act, and the Telemarketing and Consumer Fraud and Abuse Prevention Act, among others. It also publishes helpful brochures and fact sheets on topics related to the laws it enforces. Go to the FTC's Web site, *www.ftc.gov* to read its publications. You can also file a consumer complaint against a business or organization that has violated one of the laws the FTC enforces at this site, or you can make a complaint by calling 1-877-382-4357 or by writing to: Federal Trade Commission, Consumer Response Center, 600 Pennsylvania Avenue, NW, Washington, D.C. 20580.

Legal Services Corporation (LSC). This organization was established by Congress in 1974 to help ensure that all Americans, regardless of their income, have access to legal assistance. The corporation funds local programs in every state that provide legal assistance and advice to consumers who qualify for help based on their income. To learn more about the Legal Services Corporation or to locate the LSC-funded office nearest you, go to *www.lsc.gov*, call 1-202-336-8800, or write to Legal Services Corporation, 750 First Street NE, Tenth Floor, Washington, D.C. 20002-4250.